D A N C E

THE ART OF PRODUCTION

D A N C E
THE ART OF PRODUCTION

THIRD EDITION

Edited by

Joan Schlaich, B.S., M.A., Ph.D.

Betty DuPont, B.S., M.A.

Contributors

Rona Sande; Elizabeth Keen; Pat Finot and Tom Ruzika;
Ruby Abeling and Eric Ruskin; Regina Fletcher Sadono;
Doris Einstein Siegel; Virginia Freeman; Barbara Matthews;
Paul Stuart Graham and Ronald Allen-Lindblom;
Sam Dawson; Laurie Dowling

A Dance Horizons Book
Princeton Book Company, Publishers
Hightstown, NJ

A Dance Horizons Book
Princeton Book Company, Publishers
POB 831
Hightstown, NJ 08520

Library of Congress Cataloging-in-Publication Data

Dance : the art of production / edited by Joan Schlaich, Betty DuPont;
   contributors, Rona Sande . . . [et al.]. — 3rd ed.
      p.
   "A Dance Horizons Book."
   Includes bibliographical references (p.   ) and index.
   ISBN 0-87127-207-5
    1. Dance—Production and direction.   I. Schlaich, Joan.
II. DuPont, Betty.   III. Sande, Rona.
GV1782.D35   1998
792.8'0232—dc21   98-50077
                                         CIP

Printed in Canada

Contents

Preface

This new edition of *Dance: The Art of Production* has been designed to meet the needs of dance students and professionals for timely, accurate information on mounting a dance concert. It is written by experts in each area and contains specific suggestions that will guide the inexperienced and serve as a valuable checklist for the more experienced.

The book will help the director-choreographer work with theatre personnel toward a more effective concert. Moreover, all dancers should assume responsibility for a knowledge of theatrical aspects of dance production, including theatre terminology. Although most dance students are thoroughly trained in performance, many are unaware of the complexity of producing a dance concert. The Diagram of Production Personnel shows how each person relates to the others involved in mounting a dance production, with references to pertinent discussion in the chapters of the book. This chart reflects the organization used by many, but there is no set pattern that would suit all concerts or all dance companies. Many variations and job combinations are possible to cover the same production tasks.

We hope the book will help dance directors to create artistically effective as well as technically efficient dance productions, and help dancers to become more knowledgeable about the presentation of their art.

We have received much friendly help in preparing this new edition. We especially want to thank Stan Pressner for his careful reading and thoughtful comments on the lighting chapter; Andrew Milhan for his contributions to editing, updating materials, and setting up photographs; and Peter Hudson for his invaluable assistance in the preparation of the manuscript.

We are most grateful for the careful, thorough editing done by Barbara Palfy.

Joan Schlaich
Betty DuPont

1

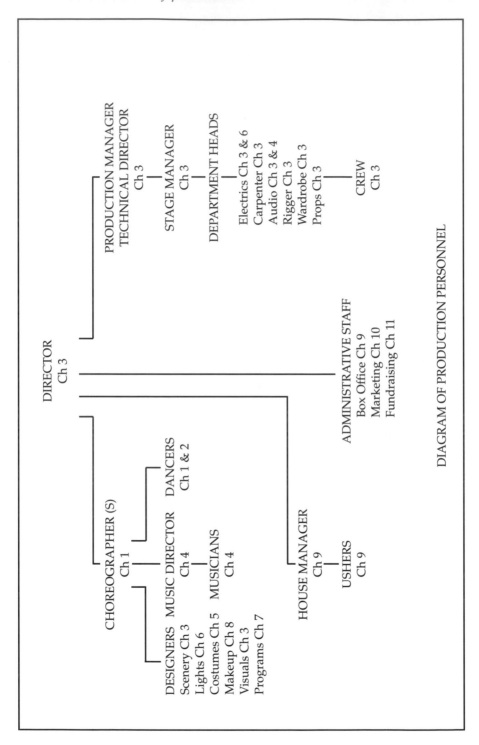

DIAGRAM OF PRODUCTION PERSONNEL

DIRECTOR
Ch 3

PRODUCTION MANAGER
TECHNICAL DIRECTOR
Ch 3

STAGE MANAGER
Ch 3

DEPARTMENT HEADS

Electrics Ch 3 & 6
Carpenter Ch 3
Audio Ch 3 & 4
Rigger Ch 3
Wardrobe Ch 3
Props Ch 3

CREW
Ch 3

ADMINISTRATIVE STAFF
Box Office Ch 9
Marketing Ch 10
Fundraising Ch 11

CHOREOGRAPHER (S)
Ch 1

DANCERS
Ch 1 & 2

MUSIC DIRECTOR
Ch 4

MUSICIANS
Ch 4

DESIGNERS
Scenery Ch 3
Lights Ch 6
Costumes Ch 5
Makeup Ch 8
Visuals Ch 3
Programs Ch 7

HOUSE MANAGER
Ch 9

USHERS
Ch 9

1 . The Experience of Dance Theatre

RONA SANDE   *Professor and Director Emeritus of Dance, University of California, Santa Barbara.*

The experience of theatre is a unique one. Its fundamental component can be the simplest of actions performed purposefully by one and observed by another in a setting designated as a stage. That is only the beginning of theatre, of course, the most basic of its elements. Yet it is an experience for both observed and observer that can be so significant as to change the lives of each.

POTENTIAL OF THEATRE

There is magic in performance. There is a certain unnamed quality that permeates the air between performers and audience, causing a communication that is possible only because of the "place" of the performers in relation to the observers. The place I am referring to is not a physical space but a psychic relationship in which the performers have in their hands the power to hold and to transform the audience by their actions. It is the experience, conscious or unconscious, of this power that compels artists to continue to perform under even the most adverse circumstances. And it is the effected transformation that brings the observers back to the theatre again and again to repeat such a meaningful experience. That is the potential of theatre.

The very concept of theatre, then, has important implications for all students of the art. The specific subjects dealt with in the chapters that follow concern the technical and practical aspects of dance production: those elements that contribute to the magic of a performance but do not by themselves constitute a production. Historically, we have seen their value and use in enhancing performance. This introduction, however, will focus on different dimensions of dance production, aspects less tangible but equally important in bringing the potential of a dance performance to its fulfillment.

DANCE-AUDIENCE RELATIONSHIP

A successful dance concert gives the audience a significant experience, whether emotionally moving, visually stimulating, kinesthetically exciting, or simply clever and entertaining. But theatrical productions sometimes have little or no effect on an audience; sometimes they do not even make a meaningful impact on the performers themselves.

The variables involved in any production are subtle and complex. Nevertheless, there are some factors, apart from those universally cited concerning excellence of choreography and its execution, that can be isolated and discussed.

Who should perform and choreograph?

One difficult problem is how to select dancers and choreographers for a performance. Young dancers desire to perform, but dance teachers have conflicting feelings in trying to uphold the standards of their art without ceasing to respect the aspirations of their students. There are, of course, some "natural" performers, but for most, performance is something that is learned, and it is learned in part from experience. Without some opportunity to perform, this ability will not be completely developed. Likewise, if a choreography is not shown to an audience, its strengths and weaknesses will never be fully illuminated.

The importance of paying careful attention to the creative and technical level of the performers and choreographers cannot be overestimated. Should anyone be allowed to perform or only the best? This question can be answered by taking a closer look at the diverse possibilities for performance.

Types of production

Different types of productions are available to serve as performing opportunities for students during their apprentice years. *Workshop*, for example, implies immediately that the production is going to be offered on a modest scale. *Demonstration* is another term commonly used to designate an informal showing of works. And there are others that denote intermediary steps before the final category of *concert*. Designations of this sort help an audience to adjust its expectations to the type of performance it is attending. Students also benefit by maintaining an accurate perspective concerning their progress in the profession. This result, however, can easily be neutralized by the uncritical responses of an audience composed largely of student colleagues and friends. (An evaluation session after the performance generally has a sobering effect.)

Times of performance

The time of performance may indicate different levels of proficiency. An evening performance is always more formal than a noon or afternoon showing of dance works, and evening audiences are more demanding. This can create a tension that is sometimes counterproductive in the first performing experiences, although these same tensions are important at a later stage.

Costumes and lighting

Elaborate costumes in a two-minute work composed of simple patterns may mislead the audience into expecting a more substantial work. The use of basic leotards and tights might be more effective. As an alternative to intricate design, imaginative use of color can distinguish the roles of dancers or divide the stage space. Similarly, complicated light plots occasionally overpower a dance.

Scaling choreography to performance

Choreography can be scaled appropriately to any performance. It is common and natural for beginners to undertake unrealistic choreographic projects beyond their technical level and the maturity of their experience. Less ambitious material can be dealt with effectively by beginning students and is just as impressive in performance. If the movements themselves are beyond the skill of the dancers, the limitations of each performer are magnified. Dancers secure in their technique can concentrate on other aspects of movement essential for performance.

Performing areas

The performing area or stage can be made anywhere. This depends solely on the desires of the choreographer or dance director. The appropriateness of the performance area can be a crucial point in determining the success or failure of a production. The possibilities are virtually endless, but this discussion is limited to the studio, the small theatre, and the large theatre.

The *studio* is the least pretentious setting for a dance perform-ance and has the advantage of providing close contact with the audi-ence. Generally this setting gives members of the audience a special feeling of good will toward the performers; perhaps the proximity of the two heightens audience responsiveness. This atmosphere is especially important for less experienced performers, who can learn a great deal about projection. A difficulty with being very close to an audience is the distraction of seeing a particular face in the fore-ground. The almost instinctive urge to acknowledge that person threatens the concentration needed for performance. Practice enables the dancer to see the audience yet project beyond the per-sonal and through the movement. The studio is an excellent place to present "first" works, previews of dances, and pilot studies of what might later become more major productions. The informality is con-ducive to the staging of experimental works and other types of dances that in their very conception demand intimacy to succeed. Often disarming in its simplicity, the studio performance generates a wonderful atmosphere.

Although the *small theatre* usually is intimate, the fact of having an actual stage, installed lights, and the other accouterments of the-atre brings higher expectations and greater formality than are com-mon in the studio. There is a special separation between the audi-ence and performers that is literal and psychological, and performers must try to bridge the gap. Still, because of the size of the theatre and the distance between audience and performers, the intensity required for projection is not overly demanding. The expe-rience is a relatively comfortable one for performers, since they do not feel the great expanse and void that can be associated with the large theatre.

The *large theatre* is the most auspicious performing space and requires greater skill on the part of the dancers in terms of projection and technique. There is an awesomeness about this performing area. When the first light appears on stage to illuminate the dancers, they are as if pinpointed in space. They look taller and bigger than they are, yet more frail and certainly more vulnerable. The human contact is yet to be made and the concentration required to establish it is more difficult and necessitates a greater expense of energy than in the other performing places. The experience of achieving this contact is the most intense and ultimately the most rewarding.

ATTITUDES TOWARD PERFORMANCE

Dancer's attitude

It is vital to stress to the dancers at the very outset the importance of working with their full concentration and with an eye toward performance at all rehearsals, even though the choreographer might be the only audience present at these sessions. To instill this attitude is seldom an easy task. The weeks and even months of intensive rehearsal needed to prepare a work for production can be deadening to the performers. The practice that leads to the more perfect execution of movement too often becomes an exercise in rote mechanical action. This is what fosters the naive attitude that "when the audience is present, spontaneity and inspiration will return." This refrain betrays a false sense of security.

There is no question that the presence of an audience affects performers. The excitement generated raises the adrenaline level of the body, and a heightened awareness results that makes the performer more alert and more sensitive than in rehearsal. But that same excitement can be the thing that destroys performance. For example, tension, never seen previously at rehearsals, suddenly becomes evident in the neck and limbs of the dancer. Balance, apparently secure in the studio, is destroyed because of nervousness. Other less subtle changes may be detected in the face of the dancer (what begins as a lively smile in rehearsal may be transformed on stage into a blank stare or even a hideous leer). But constantly stressing an "attitude of performance" during the sometimes grueling days of rehearsal makes the transference from the rehearsal studio to the stage more natural.

The performer, though deeply involved in movement, can afford the small percentage of audience consciousness necessary to good performance without detrimental "self-conscious" effects. This consciousness may result in a more sensitive performance. Moreover, each performance must be treated as a new experience. This is the responsibility of the dancer rather than the choreographer, who has already imparted the basic material of the dance. For it is the performer who must act as intermediary between the creator and the audience to exhibit the work. To do this the dancer must infuse each performance with new energy, invoking fresh images when needed to make each movement as spontaneous and inspired as it was when originally conceived.

Choreographer's attitude

As important as the attitude of the dancer toward performance is the attitude of the choreographer toward the audience. An issue that is particularly sensitive centers on the matter of responsibility of artists to their art. Dance is a performing art and as such requires the physical presence of an audience at a certain time and at a specific place (at least in its more traditional forms) to have the creative cycle completed. A performance is conceived with the idea of its being presented to (for) someone. It is especially easy for those absorbed in their work to confuse the expression of the art form with ego indulgence. Dance is perhaps the most hedonistic of the arts simply because movement in itself is a pleasurable experience. The more one becomes aware of, and sensitive to, the sensuous feedback of moving, the more one can become absorbed in the self, a danger for both choreographer and dancer. The selective eye needs always to be on guard to ensure that the joys of movement are not limited to the participants but can be transmitted to an audience, which has given up both time and money to sit in attendance.

Another barrier is an attitude of obscurantism sometimes held by the choreographer. An unwillingness to communicate in a medium that by definition is a performing art only serves to alienate the audience and thus nullify the power of dance.

ARTISTIC RESPONSIBILITIES

It is more than the exhibition of forms in time and space that makes the "experience of theatre" come alive. There is an artistic challenge and responsibility that must be met if a performance is to be successful. A dance production can vary from a casual affair to a formal extravaganza. Those involved in a production should keep in mind its purpose and treat it as an important event for both sides of the invisible curtain that separates the halves of what must ultimately become a whole.

2 . Auditions

ELIZABETH KEEN   *Dance faculty, the Juilliard School, choreographer for theatre and opera, artistic director of the Elizabeth Keen Dance Company 1966–1981.*

Auditioning offers two distinct opportunities. For the producer-director-choreographer it is a chance to find the perfect performer; for performers it is the possibility of finding the right match for their talents. Standard procedures have been developed and most auditions follow a recognizable pattern. This chapter will first examine the audition process from the point of view of the director-choreographer and then from the point of view of the performer-dancer.

CONDUCTING AUDITIONS

Planning the audition

1. First decide what sort of performers you want to attract, how much and what kind of training they should have, and how much actual performance experience. Do the available roles have particular requirements of size, appearance, temperament, and technique?
2. How many men and/or women are needed? Generally, the sexes are auditioned separately.
3. Where do you want to send your audition notice? The type of dancers you require determines whether you will send notices to studios, dance departments, or newspapers and/or trade publications.
4. What are your financial terms? Is the job for the experience only? If so, will you offer free classes? Is there performance pay only or rehearsal and performance pay? Is this a one-event engagement or a longer-term contract at a specific amount per week?
5. Where and when is the audition? Will there be one audition held locally or several in different cities? How much advance

notice do you need? What is your call-back date? Have you selected a convenient location for your call? Is your choice clean, well lit, and of an appropriate size? A decent sprung floor is a necessity and required by union rules.

6. Who helps with the audition? Have you arranged for a stage manager or the equivalent, and for a demonstrator who knows your material well? Depending on whether you use live or recorded music, you'll need a musician or sound equipment.

Announcing the audition

1. Make sure the date, place, time, and terms of the engagement are clearly stated in your notice. Briefly describe the event, production, or tour. Be specific about what kind of dancer or performer you seek; vagueness and misrepresentation waste everyone's time.
2. If your group is not well known, include some basic information about it in the announcement.
3. Notices to be posted should be designed to catch the eye. Bulletin boards are crowded and you want to make sure your information will not be overlooked.
4. If you are advertising in trade newspapers or magazines, check press deadlines.
5. Mail all notices well in advance of the audition date. Allow yourself time to contact personally acquaintances who may wish to direct dancers your way.
6. Be sure to state any specific footwear needed (i.e., pointe or tap shoes).

Mechanics of the audition*

The most efficient way to handle an audition is to separate the areas of responsibility. The director or choreographer, or both, should be solely concerned with the decisions of casting. The stage manager or equivalent should facilitate smooth operation by assuming the following responsibilities: signing people in, collecting necessary data, answering questions, aiding in communication, and keeping order.

Numbered cards to be pinned on each dancer may be distributed to facilitate identification and management. Numbered dancers can

*From the Gloria Newman chapter on Auditions in the second edition of this book.

quickly be divided into smaller groupings according to the number of applicants and time available.

Directors should keep their own records for each dancer. Many use cards with space for name, audition number, address, phone, training, and experience. The outcome of the audition may be written on the reverse side of the card. More often, however, directors will simply make use of pictures with resumés. If class is not to be included with the audition, it is helpful for dancers to have a studio available for warmup.

The movement combinations to be taught should emphasize elements the choreographer uses in the work. Standard musical theatre auditions usually begin with a ballet combination and then a jazz combination, after which the aspirants may be expected to sing, tap, or give a reading. In all areas of the business, however, the amount you ask the dancers to do obviously depends on the immediate and long-term needs. Since it is awkward to evaluate many different abilities in the same combination, design separate phrases that will demonstrate specific dancing requirements. After teaching the movement phrases in large groups, see the dancers in smaller groups, taking notes on relative abilities. It is best to eliminate quickly those you cannot use in order to focus on those you need.

Be sure applicants know when to expect the results of the audition. Should they wait that day? If not, when is the call-back? Whether you keep dancers or not, it is tremendously important to treat them courteously and to thank all of them for their time and effort.

Selecting dancers

What does a choreographer look for? At any audition the following characteristics might be evaluated:

- Individual presence, projection, and temperament
- Attitude and emotional maturity
- Physical appearance
- Technical ability
- Speed and accuracy in learning
- Ability to capture style
- Responsiveness to corrections
- Versatility or strength in specific areas
- Improvisational ability
- Related skills, such as singing, acting, playing of musical instruments, or gymnastic techniques

For a single production or individual dance, the dancer's present ability is most important. The dancer must be at the desired level of ability right now. Do not allow yourself to be sidetracked by potential, although it is a good idea to keep information on a few dancers who may be of later use. Auditioning a dancer for a company in which a long association and future development are anticipated is a different situation and provides more leeway.

Selections may be made immediately, but call-backs are advisable. Seeing a dancer a second time allows you to better assess talent and ability and gives you an opportunity to interview and check references. Much is revealed in the rehearsal process that is concealed in the audition; therefore, before making a long-term commitment to a new dancer, the choreographer should consider a trial or apprentice period. Even so, it is surprisingly easy to make a mistake. Even a very good dancer may not be right for your company; group chemistry remains a mystery.

TAKING AUDITIONS

Planning for the audition

In general, planning for an audition involves long-term training. It is the sum total of the techniques you have learned, the performance experience you have acquired, and your awareness of the field through dance history and performances you have seen. It is what you have mastered with relative ease and what you have had to struggle with. Endurance, perseverance, and guts do not develop overnight. You will need all three. Never underestimate the competition.

Specifically, planning for an audition means getting the details straight about date, time, and place. Whether you are auditioning in contemporary dance, ballet, the world of musical theatre, or industrials and commercials, it is essential to understand for whom you will dance and to dress accordingly. For example, auditioning for *A Chorus Line* in baggy sweats, an old T-shirt, and no makeup is as unintelligent as showing up in heels and sequins for a Paul Taylor call. On the other hand, if you did the latter and then instantaneously changed to black unitard, danced brilliantly, and landed a contract, you would have been noticed for what proved to be the right reasons.

Given the variety of styles in the contemporary field, modern dancers must find out as much as possible about a choreographer, either by reading, by viewing performances or videotapes, or through dancers who have already worked with the choreographer. An affinity to the particular style being asked for is key; otherwise, you may find it is beyond you or not to your taste.

If your sights are set on show business, realize that good jazz and tap techniques are only a beginning. Aim to be a triple threat: sing and act as well as dance. Currently, many dance and theatre programs have musical theatre components. If you have not been able to take advantage of them, you may need to take a year's course or study with selected teachers. Your dancing may be fine but without other skills, you will be out of the running before you begin. Most commercial auditions begin with a ballet combination to assess technical training; then a jazz combination to test your style and charisma. Since time is money, fast pick-up is prized. Appearance is also key; you cannot be too good-looking in show biz, although character has its place.

Ballet companies have their special requirements as well. Again, quick study is a necessity since there is a large repertory to learn and usually very little time in which to learn it. Versatility is a plus because of the range of styles found in most companies. An even technique, one that is strong in all areas, is preferable, and musicality is a must.

Please note that most auditions request an 8" x 10" black and white glossy head shot. Attach to the back a resume detailing your experience, training, physical essentials (height, weight, age, color eyes, clothing measurements), your name, address, telephone number and that of your agent.

Networking

Is it always whom you know? Well, not always, but often. That being so, how do you make the necessary contacts? Having ascertained which choreographer or company or production you want to aim for, the next step is to acquire or further develop the technique(s) on which the work is based. Plan to study at the school of the choreographer or company of your choice. If there is no such possibility, take workshops the choreographer or his/her dancers may teach intermittently; these often occur in summer programs. Does the group have repertory classes or a second company? Get involved. Try to get to know the dancers in the company. Take class with them. If they choreograph, try to dance with them. If you click, that can mean a recommendation. A certain amount of hanging out without presupposing connections and without becoming a doormat may be useful.

The dance world is small and interconnected. A word from one of your teachers who knows the choreographer can be helpful in singling you out from a sea of faces, although it will not get you the job. Being right for the job is what gets you the job. All the calculation in the world cannot substitute for that. Timing and luck are unquestionably important, but without skill and being good to work with, even these will not keep you in a job.

Getting through the audition

The process usually involves the following:

1. *Reading the audition notice:* This will appear on the bulletin board at a school, a studio, or in a trade paper such as *Backstage* or *Variety*. It will provide date, place, and times of audition for men and women, usually seen separately. It will also state how many positions are available, for how long, and for how much (Figure 2.1)

2. *Showing up:* For an audition, being on time means being early. You will usually be seen in the order in which you sign in with the stage manager. You want to be seen by a choreographer who is fresh and alert, not one who has already looked at hundreds of people.

3. *Warmup:* See to this ahead of time. Even if there is a warmup, it may not be the right one for you.

4. *Manners:* Good manners are essential. Be considerate of other dancers. Remember, people are observing how you relate to others as well as how you dance. Follow instructions accurately and with good will. If the group is told to place dance bags on the left side of the room, do not be the only one to put yours on the empty shelf in the back. If something goes wrong, react with humor rather than fury. Get back on track as fast as possible, just as you would cover for a mistake in a performance.

5. *Type-casting:* You may never get to dance at all, but simply be lined up with the other dancers and told to leave or stay solely on the basis of your appearance. If you are let go, this is known as being "typed out."

6. *Learning the combination(s):* Phrases are taught in large groups, then dancers are seen in smaller numbers. Accuracy is very important. Pay attention to style, nuance, and quality as well

CASTING
CHORUS CALLS

STRONG TAP, "MAKIN' WHOOPEE"

9/18 at 10AM & 2PM at the AEA Audition Center, 165 W. 46 St., 2nd fl., NYC.

An eligible performer chorus call for Houston's Theater Under The Stars production of "Makin' Whoopee" (rehearsals begin in Houston, Oct. 7; opens Nov. 1; closes Nov. 16). Frank M. Young, prod'r; Charles Repole, dir.; Dan Siretta, choreo.; Sherie L. Seff, casting dir. Chorus call procedures are in effect. Auditions will be held at the AEA Audition Center, 165 W. 46 St., 2nd fl., NYC. Dancers must bring all appropriate dance equipment and must also be prepared to sing whatever shows best vocally (standard musical comedy), absolutely no rock 'n' roll. All ethnic minorities are encouraged to attend this auditions. Non-eligible performers will be seen, time permitting. *EQ. WCLO CONTRACT.*

Thurs. Sept. 18—Eligible male dancers who sing, 10AM.

Thurs. Sept. 18—Eligible female dancers who sing, 2PM.

Seeking—Highly trained male and female dancers with strong tap who sing extremely well: all dancers must tap and must have strong musical theatre dance training.

DT "WEST SIDE STORY"

9/17 & 9/18 at 10AM & 2PM at Nola Studios, 250 W. 54 St., 11th fl., NYC.

A chorus call will be held for the Westchester Broadway Theatre (Elmsford, NY) production of "West Side Story" (first rehearsal is Oct. 27; opening Nov. 6; closing Feb. 14, with a three-week, unpaid hiatus, Dec. 8-28). Westchester Broadway Theatre, prod'r; David Cunningham, assoc. prod'r; Barry McNabb, dir./choreo.; Bill Stanley, mus'l dir. Chorus call procedures will be in effect. Auditions will be held at Nola Studios, 250 W. 54 St., 11th fl., NYC. Eligible performers of all ethnic backgrounds are encouraged to attend this audition. *EQ. DINNER THEATRE CONTRACT.*

Wed. Sept. 17—Eligible male dancers who sing, 10AM.

Wed. Sept. 17—Open call, male dancers who sing, 2PM.

Thurs. Sept. 18—Eligible female dancers who sing, 10AM.

Thurs. Sept. 18—Open call, female dancers who sing, 2PM.

Figure 2.1 Audition notice.

as steps. Even if the phrases seem impossible to pick up, do the very best you can. Your learning ability is being observed as well as your technique. You can pick up from dancers in other groups who seem to have gotten the combination as well as from the demonstrator.

7. *Asking questions:* If an explanation is muddy, you should be able to ask for clarification; however, use your judgment. Make sure you cannot figure things out on your own and that the demonstrator seems open to questioning. Disorganization in the audition also tells you something about the audition directors.

8. *Elimination:* Dancers deemed unsuitable for the job are asked to leave. Do this cheerfully even if disappointed. You are not giving the audition and do not know what they are looking for. Even if you are positive that you are the best person for the job (and you may be right) it is not the time to make a fuss.

9. *Call-backs:* Usually, the first audition is a screening process to narrow the field, and the real decisions are made at the next call. It is always important to dance your best. Practice what you have learned between calls. Never assume you have it made.

Signing the contract . . . or not

1. *Congratulations, you have the job!:* Make sure you understand the terms of the agreement: number of weeks, salary per week, travel arrangements, per diem (food and hotel allowance), dates of payment, and specific roles and duties must be included. Before, not after signing, is the time for questions. Be suspicious if the answers you receive are vague or evasive.

2. *Trial periods:* Often a company may want to try you out. This is sometimes called an apprentice period and will be specifically stated as such. Sometimes, though, you are still auditioning although no one says so. Continue to pay sharp attention. Avoid complacency. You have the job, but that does not necessarily mean you will keep it. Figuratively speaking, stay on your toes.

3. *Ouch! You do not have the job!:* The competition was strong. You lost. It is time to figure out why. Maybe others were simply better suited, more skilled, or more experienced. Maybe someone had more of an "in" than you did. Maybe you are not see-

ing yourself as others see you and need to modify your behavior or take a hard look at your dancing. Maybe, in fact, there were no positions available at all. All union companies are required by law to have open as well as union calls, even if the choreographer has already selected the dancers. Maybe, there is no discernible reason at all. You have been overlooked and have further proof that the world is unfair. So why go to these calls at all? The answer: you learn how to audition; you get a sense of the competition; you make contacts with other dancers; and you are seen. Successful productions and concert groups have more than one company. These companies may need replacements. Those who auditioned you may well remember you for future openings.

As for the here and now: at certain stages in everyone's career, involvement in one's craft is more important than money and helps to combat discouragement. Now is the time to work with your peers. If they have a success, you will move up with them. If you are able to choreograph, do so. It is a good way to be seen and puts you in the driver's seat. Seemingly insignificant gigs can prove invaluable learning opportunities, and a small job may provide the contact that leads to the next step. If you are truly serious, you will practice your craft in any reasonable way you can.

CHOREOGRAPHERS' THOUGHTS

Responses to the question, What special qualities do you look for when selecting dancers?:

Patricia Birch, choreographer, *Grease* and *Pacific Overtures* on Broadway; *First Wives' Club,* film; and *Saturday Night Live* and *The Gershwin Circle* for television.

"I like a dancer with individuality, someone who understands character and style. The dancer needs a technique appropriate to the production, but it's not all about technique. I like a dancer with an acting base."

Maria Grandy, formerly: faculty, Dance Division, the Juilliard School, Artistic Director of Joffrey II, Chairman of the Board, Dance Notation Bureau.

"I look for someone who dances with generosity and warmth. Then I look at the technique."

Benjamin Harkarvy, Artistic Director, Dance Division, the Juilliard School; founder of the Netherlands Dance Theater, and former Artistic Director of the Pennsylvania Ballet.

"I look for an intense focus when the dancers are learning the audition material. When they perform these phrases, what I hope to see, besides accuracy, is a special energy that makes me want to watch them."

Sally Hess, independent choreographer; former dancer Dan Wagoner and Dancers; faculty, Swarthmore College and Princeton University.

"I choose from dancers who take my class, from people recommended to me, or by seeing someone in performance. I say "no" to someone who isn't technically strong enough or, equally important, who isn't mentally flexible and open enough to work with me. I'm not interested in doing battle. It's not personal. It's just that some people have a mind-set about what they will and will not do, and I don't want to fight with them about what they're not willing to give. Making a dance is a joint exploration. It's a readiness to work."

Bruce Marks, Artistic Director, Boston Ballet; former Artistic Director of Ballet West; former principal dancer, American Ballet Theatre and the Royal Danish Ballet.

"Line and technical excellence are a given. The ability to reproduce choreography is a deciding factor. I also like to spend time with a prospective company member looking for a 'personality fit.' I want someone who has a love and respect for our art form and a passion for movement."

Carla Maxwell, teacher, Principal Dancer and Artistic Director, José Limón Dance Company.

"What is special to me is that dancer who has the gift of communicating ideas through movement. I go through a lengthy audition process. Our work is very process oriented. I'm concerned not only that I feel compatible with the dancer, but that the dancer is comfortable with the way our company works. From a big open call I narrow down to about twenty dancers who are invited to a workshop of technique and repertory classes. I look for musicality, phrasing, and a grasp of the sense of the choreography. I observe how the dancers take direction and if they are able to change. I look for a clean style—too many personal mannerisms are difficult to deal with—but not one that is boring or without personality. I need vital, passionate movers. After a week, the dancers are asked to perform individually what they've learned in rep as well as to present a solo that they already know well. The choice they make here is always very interesting. It shows me where they come from and where they are as artists. I need an ensemble of soloists; there can be no filler. The dancers chosen have to commit to being a part of the company. It's not just a job."

Paul Taylor, choreographer and Artistic Director, the Paul Taylor Dance Company.

"I look at the eyes. I look to see if it's someone I'd like to work with. Not just eyes, but general demeanor . . . if they're polite to one another; if they say excuse me when they bump. Technique and experience aside, I look for someone I'd really like to work with over the years, as a person as well as a dancer. This [modern dance] business isn't one hundred percent business. It's a family, a professional family."

3 . Technical Theatre: Its Relationship to Dance Theatre

PAT FINOT *Professor of dance and production coordinator, Department of Dance, California State University, Long Beach.*

TOM RUZIKA *Lecturer in design, University of California, Irvine. Principal Designer, The Ruzika Company.*

The theatre is a wonderful place. It is a place where dance magic can happen, but this magic cannot be made with magic. The theatre is a complicated place and requires complicated planning. If this is not done, the theatre becomes a place of frustration and headaches and is no longer wonderful. The magic of dance theatre starts in the creative imagination of the choreographer and develops through the careful forethought, preplanning, and execution of many creative artists.

From the moment the choreographer starts a new work, technical theatre considerations should be a part of the thought processes. This then implies that the choreographer must have at least a rudimentary knowledge of how a theatre works. The student of choreography should have classwork in lighting design and execution, sound reproduction, set design and construction, and theatre management—and all dance students should have practical experience working on a dance theatre technical crew.

Probably one of the primary reasons that the work of Alwin Nikolais was so tremendously satisfying was because in concept and in execution it was the work of one man. Nikolais was a choreographer, a composer, and a set, lighting, and costume designer. This means that his original idea never had to undergo a process of assimilation and translation to be executed by someone else. Therefore, the end product was the direct result of a single person bringing his concepts to life.

As few people have the technical knowledge and artistic background to execute their ideas in all of these areas, the problem becomes one of communication. If others are to design from choreographers' images, the choreographers must be able to make themselves understood in the terms of other elements. This communication takes place on two levels: (1) through the dance itself; and (2) through the verbal communication of the choreographer to the lighting designer, set designer, composer, and costumer. This communication is possible only if choreographers know enough about the designers' fields, artistically and practically, to make themselves understood, hence making the work of the designers both possible and artistically satisfying.

The ideal combination is an artistically sound choreographer-director with a practical knowledge of technical theatre working closely with qualified lighting and set designers and a well-organized stage crew under the direction of a skilled stage manager who is knowledgeable in the area of dance.

CONCERT PREPLANNING

The most important factor governing the amount of work that will be involved in the production of any dance concert is the determination of where the dances will be performed. Planning a dance concert choreographed by a group of college students to be performed in their own dance studio is quite different from planning a dance concert that will tour the nation. Acting as sponsor to a traveling dance company also takes special knowledge. Therefore, the production of dance concerts falls into three basic categories:

1. Dances designed for an "at home" facility, involving schools, studios, and theatres
2. Dances to be toured, involving a variety of theatres, studios, and other performance areas
3. Booking and sponsoring traveling dance companies

In any of these categories, attention must be paid to technical theatre considerations when contracts are signed or agreements are made (see Sample Worksheets 3.1 and 3.2). All contracts or agreements should cover:

- All necessary technical theatre equipment
- All technical theatre personnel
- Specifically scheduled theatre time (setup, rehearsal, and performance)

SAMPLE WORKSHEET 3.1
Technical Production Contract Requirements for Touring Dance Companies: Major Theatre Concerts

THE SPONSOR AGREES TO SUPPLY OR CAUSE TO BE SUPPLIED TO THE COMPANY, AT SPONSOR'S EXPENSE, THE FOLLOWING PRODUCTION REQUIREMENTS:

1. FACILITY
   a. Company requires a proscenium theatre space with resilient floor (no concrete). A minimum dance area of 40' width at the proscenium and 30' depth is required, plus upstage crossover. There must also be sufficient clear wing space.
   b. Performance space heated to 71–75 degrees Fahrenheit.
   c. Stage floor and offstage wing space shall be in a clean and safe dance condition.
   d. Stage area shall be exclusively available to the Company and not used by any other event during the period that the Company occupies the premises.
   e. Adequate and secure storage space shall be provided, if required.

2. RIGGING AND MASKING
   a. Complete set of black legs and borders to mask the stage. Masking must be set according to the specifications provided by the Company prior to its arrival.
   b. Upstage white cyc, black scrim and black velour. Wrap-around cycloramas cannot be used.
   c. Main act curtain.

3. WARDROBE
   a. Dressing room space adjacent to the stage for 10 female dancers and 4 male dancers.
   b. Dressing rooms shall be clean, heated, and equipped with tables, mirror, lights, chairs, hot and cold running water, and costume racks.
   c. Laundry facilities shall be conveniently available to the Company.
   d. Company shall have exclusive use of the dressing rooms during its residency.

4. PROPERTIES
   a. The Company will provide its own vinyl dance floor.
   b. (4) 6' by 3' prop tables to be positioned stage left and stage right.
   c. A tuned grand piano is required in the orchestra pit.
   d. (6) music stands and lights located offstage.
   e. (20) straight-back orchestra chairs located offstage.

SAMPLE WORKSHEET 3.1 (Continued)

5. LIGHTING
   a. The Sponsor shall provide the Company with complete scale drawings (plan and section) of the performance space. "Working" equipment and inventory lists shall also be provided.
   b. The Company shall provide a detailed lighting plot which must be hung, circuited, and patched prior to the arrival of the Company. The Company will directly supervise the focusing and cuing of the equipment.
   c. Equipment must not be altered or changed once it has been set by the Company for the performance.
   d. Minimum equipment required (exact specifications will be provided on the "Hanging Plot"):
      (125) ellipsoidal spotlights
      (25) fresnels
      (5) cyc strips
      (8) 8' booms with 32 standard sidearms
      (48) dimmers
      cable, gel frames, ladders
   e. Color filters will be provided by the Company.

6. AUDIO
   a. Headset communication to all technical areas of the space.
   b. PA amplifier and house speaker system with one hand-held microphone, stand, and 25' cable.
   c. The Company will provide its own tape deck, amplifier, mixer, and speaker system. Sponsor shall provide all necessary electrical outlets and connections to power the equipment.
   d. Company reserves the right to make use of all, or a part, of the performance facility's audio system if Company so desires.

7. PERSONNEL
   a. An appointed representative of the Sponsor with decision-making authority shall always be present when the Company occupies the facility.
   b. Crew call requirements:
      Initial rigging and electrics hang (prior to Company's arrival):
         Electrics: 8 persons @ 8 hours
         Riggers: 2 persons @ 8 hours
         Carpenters: 2 persons @ 4 hours
      Load-in, set-up, and focus (upon Company's arrival):
         Loaders: 2 persons @ 2 hours
         Riggers: 2 persons @ 4 hours

SAMPLE WORKSHEET 3.1 (Continued)

Electrics: 6 persons @ 4 hours
Carpenters: 2 persons @ 4 hours
Props: 2 persons @ 4 hours
Audio: 1 person @ 4 hours
Wardrobe: 1 person @ 4 hours
Rehearsal and performance calls:
  Riggers: 1 person
  Electrics: 4 persons
  Carpenters: 1 person
  Props: 1 person
  Audio: 1 person
  Wardrobe: 1 person
Strike and load-out (of Company's equipment):
  Loaders: 2 persons @ 2 hours
  Riggers: 2 persons @ 2 hours
  Electrics: 4 persons @ 2 hours
  Carpenters: 2 persons @ 2 hours
  Props: 2 persons @ 2 hours
  Audio: 1 person @ 2 hours
  Wardrobe: 1 person @ 2 hours
c. The same crew members shall be assigned to work all rehearsal and performance calls.

THE SPONSOR AGREES TO COMPLETE THE ENCLOSED FACILITIES QUESTIONNAIRE AND RETURN IT TO THE COMPANY WITHIN 5 DAYS OF EXECUTION OF THE PERFORMANCE CONTRACT AGREEMENT.

In schools it is wise to double-check for classes that may meet in the theatre during the scheduled rehearsal time. It is generally a good idea not to schedule a dance production concurrently with any other productions in the theatre. Most often, lighting and other setup needs will be so different that someone will have to compromise beyond the point of artistic return.

Another important consideration when entering contracts and agreements is the budget. Someone has to pay for the following:

• Designer
• Music director

SAMPLE WORKSHEET 3.2
Technical Production Contract Requirements for Touring
Lecture Demonstrations: Gymnasiums or Small Theatres

THE SPONSOR AGREES TO SUPPLY OR CAUSE TO BE SUPPLIED TO
THE COMPANY, AT SPONSOR'S EXPENSE, THE FOLLOWING PRO-
DUCTION REQUIREMENTS:

1. FACILITY
   a. Resilient floor (no concrete) in a clean, safe dance condition. Minimum
      size of 30' wide by 25' deep.
   b. Performance areas and offstage areas clean and heated to 71–75 degrees
      Fahrenheit.
   c. Masking, if needed.
   d. Parking passes adjacent to the performance space.
2. WARDROBE AND PROPS
   a. Access to clean and heated dressing rooms.
   b. (2) 6' × 3' tables to be positioned stage left and stage right.
   c. Tuned grand piano.
   d. Podium.
3. LIGHTING
   a. Note: some gymnasium performances may use existing light.
   b. No less than (12) instruments (ellipsoidal spotlights or PAR 64 spots)
      depending on size of performance space.
   c. (4) light boom towers, 10' minimum height.
   d. Minimum (6) 2.4kw dimmers, sufficient cable for connections.
   e. Access to all other equipment.
4. AUDIO
   a. Tape deck and amplifier system.
   b. At least two speakers, depending on the size of performance area.
   c. PA amplifier and speaker system with one hand-held microphone,
      stand, and 25' cable.
   d. Communication system, if needed.
5. PERSONNEL
   a. An appointed representative of the Sponsor with decision-making
      authority shall always be present when the Company occupies the
      facility.
   b. Crew call requirements:
      Load-in, set-up, and rehearsal
         General stagehands: 4 persons @ 2 hours
      Performance and load-out
         General stagehands: 4 persons @ 2 hours
   c. The same crew members shall be assigned to work all rehearsal and
      performance calls.

THE SPONSOR AGREES TO COMPLETE THE ENCLOSED FACILITIES
QUESTIONNAIRE AND RETURN IT TO THE COMPANY WITHIN 5 DAYS
OF EXECUTION OF THE PERFORMANCE CONTRACT AGREEMENT.

- Stage manager
- Stage crew
- Other support as required by the institution
- Materials for sets, sound, and special effects
- Rental of equipment not owned by the institution
- Lighting supplies: color media and lamps
- Piano tuning

This list is only a general outline; every situation is different, both as to the amount of the charges and as to who pays for them.

In a union house the crew might work on a minimum four-hour call but do only the jobs specified in their contract. For example, a fly-person in a union house can do nothing but operate the rigging equipment (flown scenery or curtains). If something is flown just once, that is all the flyperson can do; the flyperson may not help focus lights but must be paid for the full four-hour minimum. Also, some professional houses charge for the use of each piece of equipment.

The situation in a college or university is generally very different. Often there is little or no charge for the use of the theatre or technical equipment. In many instances the technical crew will consist of students from the dance or theatre departments working for class credit. In some circumstances paid crews will be required. Artistic and management personnel may be faculty, staff, graduate students, or guest artists. Sometimes, substantial fees are involved for their services.

A professional dance company generally pays its own designers, sound technicians, and stage manager. The company will ordinarily carry its own sets, sound tapes, wardrobe, and color media. Some companies also carry their own sound reproduction equipment, special lighting instruments, and projection equipment. The sponsoring organization generally pays for the stage crew, other support staff, and all basic lighting instruments and sound equipment. Often the sponsoring organization also has to pay for the rental of any equipment specified by the company.

As soon as the contracts or agreements have been completed, whoever is in charge of the technical aspects of the dance production should immediately begin investigating the specifications of the theatre or other performance area. When an institution is sponsoring its own concert, talks should start immediately to determine what will be technically feasible to produce in the performance space. If a company is planning to travel and perform in many different theatres, a facilities questionnaire should be sent well in advance of the performance dates to every theatre in which it will play. The facilities questionnaire asks questions about every technical aspect of a theatre and is often used as a supplement to the contract (see Sample Worksheet 3.3). Any institution that books traveling dance companies should be prepared to have available, in writing, all technical information concerning its performance areas.

TECHNICAL THEATRE PERSONNEL[*]

Production manager or event manager

Many theatre organizations, especially educational theatres and civic theatres, employ production managers or event managers who are responsible for booking, scheduling, and budgeting the theatre facility. These individuals are usually the main contact for the dance company that is using the facility. The production manager is usually the supervisor of the theatre's technical staff. All negotiations for the use of theatre space are coordinated by the production manager or event manager.

Technical director

Each theatre generally has a technical director. This is the person who is ultimately responsible for the theatre and who ordinarily has the last word on what can or cannot be done in the theatre. Technical theatre arrangements and final production coordination are generally handled through this person. In many institutions the technical director also assumes all the responsibilities of the lighting and set designers and stage manager.

Stage manager

Stage managers are in charge of all technical aspects of the show. They must know the dances thoroughly, including all details of the movement, music, lighting, sets, and costumes. They are in charge from the time the company steps into the theatre until it leaves. It is up to the stage manager to coordinate all aspects of what will

---

[*]See Diagram of Production Personnel (Preface, p. 2), which shows how these various functions interrelate.

SAMPLE WORKSHEET 3.3
Facilities Questionnaire

BOOKING
Sponsor/Producer _____ Telephone _____ Name of Theatre
_____ Address of Theatre _____ Telephone _____ Technical
Supervisor _____ Telephone _____ Seating Capacity of House _____
Advertised time of performance _____

STAGE
Width of proscenium _____ Distance from apron line to curtain line _____
Depth from curtain line to upstage backdrop _____ Is there a pit elevator?
_____ Dimensions of orchestra pit _____ Can pit be raised to form an
extended apron? _____ Depth from front of pit to apron line _____ Is there
an upstage crossover? _____ Loading door access _____ Type of piano _____
Is theatre/house used as a classroom? _____

FLOOR
What type of material on surface? _____

RIGGING, DRAPES, AND MASKING
Is there fly space? _____ Height of gridiron _____ Available flylines _____
Usual trim on overhead masking _____ Usual trim on electric pipes _____
Color of house masking curtains _____ How many sets of legs and borders?
_____ Muslin cyc _____ Scrim cyc _____ Plastic cyc _____ White scrim
_____ Blue scrim _____ Black scrim _____ Upstage black velour _____
Is main act curtain electric or manual? _____

DRESSING ROOMS AND WARDROBE
Are quick change rooms close the to stage? _____ Are showers available?
_____ Do student classes use the dressing rooms? _____ Are laundry
facilities available on site? _____

AUDIO
Location of audio control _____ Type of mixer, amplifier, and speaker system
_____ Type of tape deck _____ Number of portable speakers _____ Type
of wiring connections on speakers _____ Is there a headset system? _____ Is
there a monitoring/paging system? _____

LIGHTING
Location of control console _____ Type of control console _____ Type of
dimming system _____ Number and wattage of dimmers _____ Type of
patch system _____ If patch panel, number of inputs per dimmer _____
Front of house hanging positions _____ Over the stage hanging positions
_____ Type of connectors _____ Manufacturer(s) of instruments _____ 5°
ellipsoidals _____ 10° ellipsoidals _____ 15° ellipsoidals _____ 20°
ellipsoidals _____ 30° ellipsoidals _____ 40° ellipsoidals _____ 50°

SAMPLE WORKSHEET 3.3 (Continued)

ellipsoidals _____ 6" fresnels _____ 8" fresnels _____ Par spots (WFL/ MFL/VNSP) _____ Beam projectors _____ Strips/borders (number of circuits) _____ Cyc lights (number of circuits) _____ Followspots _____ Effects projectors _____ Projection equipment _____ Tophats, barndoors _____ Cable, twofers, adaptors _____

CREW
Is theatre a union house? _____ Paid non-union crew _____ Paid student crew _____ Student crew related to a class _____ Volunteer crew _____ Required meal break hours _____ Academic class conflicts _____

---

become the show, which includes developing and executing the total schedule that meets all personnel and performance needs.

Stage managers "run the show," that is, they call every technical cue in the show. In calling the cues the stage manager has to give all members of the crew (lights, sound, scenery, and floor crew) adequate warning time so that the final "go" is exactly timed and "on cue." It is also the stage manager's responsibility to cue the dancers so that they are in the proper place at the proper time.

Safety is another responsibility of the stage manager. The theatre is a potentially dangerous place and items such as running lights, safety cables, glow tape, and floor conditions must be checked by the stage manager to reduce the risk of injury to all backstage personnel.

The stage manager is the main line of communication between the dancers and the technical personnel; between "backstage" and the front of the house. The house manager coordinates the work of the ticket window, ticket takers, ushers, and other staff responsible for upkeep of the auditorium and lobby of the theatre (see Chapter 9 for a detailed description of house management). The stage manager and the house manager decide when the show starts.

Stage managers who tour with professional dance companies are generally in charge of all technical theatre prearrangements and hence it is their responsibility to make sure that the theatre is ready when the company arrives. When on the road the stage manager must be flexible, able to adapt to different terms for the same thing (e. g., beam, antepro, ceiling slot, front of the house) and to different equipment and physical setups. The stage manager should be prepared for any eventuality (see Sample Worksheet 3.4).

SAMPLE WORKSHEET 3.4
Stage Manager's Production Aids

Whether on the road or at a "home" performance, a stage manager should have the following items readily available for use:

First-aid kit	Scissors
Ice packs	Magnetic clips
Large and small clipboards	Stapler, paper clips, rubber bands
Lighted clipboard	Padlocks
Stopwatch	Sewing supplies
High-intensity gooseneck lamp	50-foot measuring tape
Flashlights	Oil, small can
Gray gel (for eliminating glare from any unwanted light source)	Architects scale rule, drafting supplies
Tool kit (carpentry and miscellaneous)	Spray adhesive, white glue
Tape: masking, gaffers, double-sided, electrical, spike, "glo"	Audio supplies: adapters, connectors
Soldering iron and solder	Zip cord
Work gloves, hard hat	Extension cord
Paper towels	Candles and matches
Additional blank cue sheets	Portable label printer
Pencils, erasers, paper, chalk, felt-tip pens, grease pencils, file folders	Laptop computer with word processing, database, calendar schedule, drafting, and lighting paperwork software
Portable computer printer	

It is important to note that most stage managers have more experience calling stage plays and musicals than dance. It is up to the choreographer to realize this and allow time for the stage manager to become familiar with the movement. Some excellent theatre stage managers cannot read movement cues easily, whereas others can read them rapidly. Therefore, the choreographer-director should not be surprised to find that the time needed for familiarization with a dance may vary greatly from one stage manager to another. It is a great help to give the stage manager videotapes of the dances prior to theatre rehearsals.

The stage manager and the lighting designer may or may not be one and the same person. Both jobs can be done by one person when touring a dance production, and this simply eliminates another "translation" process.

Good stage managers are very special people. They must know technical theatre and, just as important, they must be able to work with people—stage crew, the director, and the dancers. This is not always easy, but there is much that the dancers and choreographer-director can do to make it easier.

Lighting designer

Lighting directors are creative artists and should have the technical knowledge to know how their designs can be executed. They should know whether their designs will be fairly easy to do in a given situation or whether they will be difficult and time-consuming. Good theatre lighting designers are not necessarily good designers for dance. Lighting designers for dance must intuitively see what needs to be highlighted, what needs to be underplayed, and what needs to be molded. *A good lighting designer will know what effects will work and how to achieve them far better than most choreographers.*

Not all lighting designers will be able to work well with all choreographers, no matter how competent both parties are. As with the selection of any other artistic personnel (composer, costume designer, and set designer), the choreographer and the lighting designer must have a similar artistic sense. They must have respect for each other's artistic ability and be able to think along parallel lines to achieve an artistically whole production. Therefore, it is generally best if the choreographer and lighting designer have seen each other's work before starting to collaborate.

Lighting designers produce the light plots, instrument schedules, cue schedules, and special effects. It is their responsibility to keep accurate records so that a dance can be easily recreated. These records should be made available for the company or dance department files.

Set designer

The set designer often both designs and builds sets and other decor for dance. This person needs a thorough knowledge of technical theatre, movement, and the materials of the craft. As sets for dance are often an intrinsic part of a dance, not just decor, it is important that the choreographer and set designer start working together long before the performance. It is usually desirable that the sets be completed before a dance is begun because they may have to be modified after the dancers have experimented with them. This process generally ensures the most fully integrated use of sets and movement.

The set designer should work closely with the stage manager, making sure that there is adequate performance and storage space and planning for the necessary personnel to handle the sets. When sets are designed for a touring company, additional limitations are imposed, as the sets must be reasonably lightweight, compact, and easily assembled and broken down.

The set designer must also work very closely with the lighting designer to ensure artistic unity in the work.

Music director

The music director is responsible for all aspects of producing live and recorded sound. Often this person fills four roles: composer; performer; music adviser; sound technician. (See Chapter 4 for more on the role of a music director.)

The music director must be able to work with the director, stage manager, and choreographers. The responsibility of integrating sound into the smooth running of the show includes selection of appropriate music, coordination of personnel and equipment, making of the master tape and rehearsal and standby tapes, setting of levels, and identification of cues. Consistently high-quality sound is of great importance to any dance concert. It is also essential that the special needs of dancers be met. For example, backstage speakers are generally a necessity so that dancers can hear.

When a music director is not available, an audio technician is responsible for the technical aspects of sound production.

Costume designer

The costume designer designs and often constructs the costumes. The color and the light-absorbing or light-reflective quality of fabric are distinctly design-technical considerations. These elements must be considered in relation to the sets and lighting design, requiring communication among all designers before construction begins. (See Chapter 5 for more on costuming.)

Stage crew

The stage crew includes all backstage personnel working under the direction of the stage manager. If working in a union house, crew members theoretically should be highly skilled in their areas of specialization and on duty during the entire time for which they are called. School situations, however, may be vastly different. In many theatres a number of students will be appointed to "crew" a production. Sometimes they are theatre students who are accustomed to working plays rather than dance performances. Other times they are dance students who know nothing about technical theatre. In any case, it is important to be aware that crews often have to be trained in the procedures of running a dance performance.

Another problem commonly encountered in working with student crews is that most of the time, and usually at the wrong time, students have to go to class. It is not unusual to have a crew disappear without warning right in the middle of a lighting setup. In other instances a class will be the crew. This is a real problem, as it generally means that a working crew will be available only during the regular scheduled class time. It is tremendously important that the same crew work both the rehearsals and the performance. Therefore, these scheduling problems should be made known and solved during the initial agreement period. If they are not, unwanted "surprises" can destroy the most highly organized dance group.

The stage crew requirements depend on the complexity of the production (see Sample Worksheet 3.5). Production crews are normally divided into "departments," each supervised by a "department head." The basic areas of responsibility for each department are the following:

- ELECTRICS
    Hang and focus lights
    Control console operation
    Followspot operations
    Special electrical effects
    Gel changes
    Music stand and running lights

- CARPENTERS
    Scenery and masking setup
    Scenery shifting (wagon or platform movement)
    Motorized scenery operation

SAMPLE WORKSHEET 3.5
Technical Schedule and Crew Planning Guide

1. MAJOR TOURING CONCERTS
   a. Theatre preparation, rigging, electrics hang: 8 hours/6 persons
   b. Company equipment load-in: 2 hours/4 persons
   c. Lighting focus: 4 hours/4 persons
   d. Company spacing and cuing rehearsal: 4 hours/6 persons
   e. Company class: 30 minutes to 1 hour
   f. Performance calls: 3 hours/6 persons
   g. Company warm-down: 15 to 30 minutes
   h. Company equipment load-out: 2 hours/4 persons
   i. House equipment strike: 4 hours/6 persons

2. NEW WORKS/MAJOR PREMIERES
   a. Technical rehearsals: 1½ to 2 hours per dance
   b. Special effects (scenery, rigging, lighting, makeup, costumes, props): 1 to 3 hours per effect
   c. Photo call: 1½ to 2 hours

3. LECTURE DEMONSTRATIONS
   a. Theatre preparation: 2 hours/4 persons
   b. Company spacing/technical rehearsal: 2 hours/4 persons
   c. Performance call: 1 hour/4 persons
   d. Company load-out: 1 hour/4 persons

- RIGGERS
   All flyline movement
   Rig counterweighting
   Main act curtain

- PROPS
   Set, hand, and dressing props
   Mechanical sound effects
   Orchestra (music stand) setup
   Dance floor installation
   Floor mopping and sweeping
   Tech table setter

- AUDIO
   All electronic sound effects (taped and reinforced)
   Speaker placement
   Microphone placement
   Control console operation

- WARDROBE
  Costume issuing
  Costume maintenance
  Dressing

- LOADERS
  Load and unload trucks (only)

TECHNICAL CONSIDERATIONS FOR DANCE

When mounting a new work for a specific theatre or prior to taking an existing work into an unfamiliar theatre, the choreographer-director and stage manager should be aware of the effect of the following technical considerations on the performance of the dance:

- STAGE SPACE
  Stage opening (proscenium opening)
  Depth of stage
  Backstage crossover space
  Type, size, and color of masking pieces
  Background scrim, cyclorama, backdrop, and curtain
  Type and condition of floor surface
  Space for stage manager to see and call the show
  Any unusual conditions

- COSTUMES
  Dressing-room facilities
  Quick-change areas on or near the stage
  Facilities for storing and locking clothes and valuables
  Facilities for laundering, repairing, and ironing clothes

- SETS
  Stage space
  Type of overhead grid system (type of fly system)
  Load-in facilities
  Storage space
  Availability of "shop" equipment
  Any unusual conditions

- LIGHTS
  Manufacturer, type, specifications, and availability of all equipment
  Placement and safety of on-stage lighting equipment

Availability and type of color media
Location of control equipment

- SOUND

  Manufacturer, type, specifications, and availability of all
  equipment
  Existing communications systems
  Location of speakers
  Location of control equipment

- PROJECTIONS

  Manufacturer, type, specifications, and availability of all
  equipment
  Dimensions of the performance area as it relates to placement
  of projectors
  Surfaces to be projected upon

- SPECIAL EFFECTS

  Special laws or codes concerning fires, flames, smoke, and
  explosions
  Safety of all personnel and audience
  Experimentation time needed to perfect an effect

- MUSIC

  Number of musicians required
  Union requirements
  Performance location of musicians
  Instrument requirements
  Rehearsal requirements
  Audio requirements

- VIDEO

  Number of technicians required
  Number of cameras and equipment required
  Camera location
  Shooting schedule
  Lighting requirements
  Union requirements (dancers, technicians, musicians)

- CREW/SCHEDULE

  Union, nonunion, or student crew
  Facility/class schedule
  Student class commitments

Minimum crew call requirements
Meal break requirements

INFLUENCE OF TECHNICAL THEATRE ON THE
CHOREOGRAPHIC PROCESS

If the choreographer knows the theatre in which the work will be presented, the list of technical considerations should be reviewed during the choreographic process. This will save theatre rehearsal time and eliminate the need to rechoreograph because of the limitations of the theatre. For example, if the floor is full of splinters it would be senseless to choreograph slides, knee turns, and such. Fortunately, this problem is generally solved by the purchase of a relatively inexpensive, portable roll-down vinyl dance floor.

The size of the apron (the stage floor in front of the proscenium opening) is also important. If there is an apron, even if it cannot be lighted, the performing space is usable right up to the curtain line. If there is no apron or a very small one, the dancers will have to stay well behind the curtain line. If there is an enormous apron, the dancers can use it provided it can be lighted; otherwise they will appear to be dancing in a hole. As there are generally no side entrances to an apron, movement would have to be designed without downstage entrances and exits. Some aprons are removable; however, this is usually a time-consuming job.

The number, placement, and size of masking legs (curtains) as well as the number and size of lighting instruments to be placed behind the legs also affect the choreographic process. A useful technique is to reproduce the floor plan of the legs and instruments on the rehearsal floor with masking tape. This will ensure that the dancers will be accustomed to the stage space and to its exits and entrances and that they will have adequate time for fast reentrances.

Backstage crossovers become crucial when dances are choreographed to exit one side of the stage and enter from the other. The time to make the crossing is easily calculated where a crossover exists. However, when a dancer must go outside and around a building, down a flight of stairs, through a parking lot, and back up an elevator (with the distinct possibility of being locked out on the other side), it would be wise to forget the whole thing or to take a dancer and stopwatch and time the entire procedure. With the development of more and more thrust stages, three-quarter round stages, and theatres in the round, many touring companies are including works in their repertory that require no internal exits or entrances whatsoever.

The grid system becomes very important when sets are designed to be flown. Although theatres are designed to be flexible, most are not so flexible that sets, drapes, or other decor can be flown anywhere. The exact placement of available battens for flying may also be taped on the studio floor, thus allowing the choreographer to space the dancers accurately. Backstage space is a vital consideration when large sets must be stored or when a large number of dancers are used. Some theatres have very little backstage space and large sets would make it impossible for dancers to maneuver in the area.

It is important to know if a theatre owns scrims or other drapes needed for special effects before designing them into a dance. Many a budget has been shattered by the last-minute need to rent such equipment—the basic lighting capacity of a theatre is important. If an area of the stage cannot be lighted, that area is not usable performance space. Although a theatre should have enough instruments to cover the entire stage space, it is not unusual to find that the last three or four feet upstage are in darkness. This cannot always be remedied by renting instruments, as sometimes the dimmer board is not capable of handling additional equipment.

A word of warning about tape decks: in both school and professional company situations it is highly desirable to use the same tape deck for all rehearsals and for performance. Tape decks, no matter how carefully calibrated, may vary slightly in speed. Even though slight, this variation is often enough to take the sparkle and polish off the dance performance.

ORGANIZING TECHNICAL REHEARSALS

Prior to going into the theatre, it is necessary that all schedules be confirmed by all personnel. This includes theatre times, crew and dancer calls, and arrangements with any other personnel needed for the production (see Sample Worksheet 3.5). Before the dancers arrive for rehearsals the stage needs to be readied. The stage facilities should be clean and neat; all settings or equipment in the performance area should be removed.

The lighting instruments should be hung according to the lighting designer's specifications. Many touring companies have a "universal" light plot that will adapt to almost any theatre. It is customary for these plots to be sent to the host theatre several weeks prior to the performance, and it is expected that the lights will be completely hung by the time the company arrives. The focusing of the lighting instruments will then be carried out by the lighting designer or stage manager. It saves a great deal of wear and tear on the dancers when this can be done without them. This is possible only when the dancers are predictably accurate in their spacing and when the stage manager is thoroughly familiar with the dance. It is almost never possible when mounting a new work.

Often a cue-to-cue rehearsal follows the focusing of the lights. As the name implies, this is a stage-crew rehearsal that is run directly from one cue to the next without dancers or music. At this time, light levels are set while the light-board operator learns what operations are to be performed for the order, execution, and timing of light cues. A sequential numbering system is assigned to all cues. Also at this time members of the floor crew learn their gel changes. To do this "stage walkers" are needed, and costumes for each dance should be available for a light check. Dancers can be used for this process if there is good coordination between dancers and the lighting personnel. Experienced dancers can mark their spacing while the stage manager or lighting designer adjusts the light levels on them, thus accomplishing two things at once and saving time. As the dancers walk through for spacing they will determine which entrances and exits to use and "spike marks" (see Glossary) may be used for particularly difficult placement

At this time any special lighting cues can be worked out with the dancers. This method of combining lighting and spacing rehearsal should be used only after considering dancer experience, crew experience, and time schedules. Often the wisest process is to set the lighting levels, have the dancers space, and then work out special light cues with the dancers and correct lighting problems created by spacing changes.

Prior to the technical rehearsal, all sound levels should be set. Sometimes this can be done during the cue-to-cue rehearsal. To set the levels, the stage manager and choreographer or artistic director should walk throughout the house and indicate to the sound technician the proper degree of loudness for the sound. In an unfamiliar house it is a good idea to ask the technical director if there are any "dead spots" or "live spots," as they should be avoided when setting levels. It is generally not necessary to run the entire performance tape when setting levels, but the sound for each dance should be spot-checked. This is another job that can be done prior to the dancers' arrival. The sound levels on the stage should be checked to make sure that the dancers will be able to hear.

If the preceding steps have been followed, the technical rehearsal should run fairly smoothly. The purpose of a technical rehearsal is to give the stage crew the opportunity to run through the entire show. It is at this time that the timing of cues should become accurate. Consequently, the emphasis here is on technical theatre considerations and time must be allowed for the correction of any technical problems. Choreographic or dancer performance problems are secondary in a technical run-through. Only performance problems directly caused by technical considerations should be solved at this time; all other performance notes should be given to the dancers only at the breaks.

Dress rehearsals should be run *exactly as the show will be run*. All costumes, props, makeup, sets, and special effects should be used. There should be no stops, even if a major problem occurs, and intermissions should be timed accurately. The only reason for stopping would be the occurrence of a physically dangerous situation. The need for this rehearsal cannot be overemphasized. Anyone who has run a concert without a proper dress rehearsal will be able to tell many stories about "what happened when!" The same personnel should be used in the cue-to-cue, technical, and dress rehearsals and the actual performance.

THE TIMING OF TECHNICAL REHEARSALS

Determining the time for all aspects of mounting a concert in a theatre is difficult because so many variables are involved. In a well-run house it would be expected that the previous show would be struck and that the stage would be clear, clean, and organized prior to the dance company's scheduled time in the theatre.

Depending on the clarity of the light plot, complexity of the show, size of the crew, and number of hours assigned to work, it should take one to two days to hang the show. Focusing the show may take four hours or a day, again depending on the complexity of the show. A cue-to-cue rehearsal may take one to four hours, depending on the experience of the crew. Spacing the dances may take an hour or a day, depending on the experience of the dancers and the relation of the rehearsal space to the stage space. Light levels may be set simultaneously or may be done separately, generally taking one to five hours. It should take only about a half-hour to set sound levels.

SAMPLE WORKSHEET 3.6
Production Schedule: "New Works" Dance Concert

Friday	June 1	1p–5p	Clear stage, rig masking and scenery
		5p–6p	Dinner
		6p–10p	Hang electrics
Saturday	June 2	9a–1p	Hang electrics
		1p–2p	Lunch
		2p–6p	Focus electrics
		6p–7p	Dinner
		7p–11p	Focus electrics
Sunday	June 3	9a–11a	Tech dance #1
		11a–1p	Tech dance #2
		1p–2p	Lunch
		2p–3:30p	Tech Dance #3
		3:30p–5p	Tech dance #4
		5p–6:30p	Tech dance #5
		6:30p–8p	Dinner
		8p–9:30p	Tech dance #6
		9:30p–11p	Tech dance #7
Monday	June 4	5p–7p	Tech preparation
		7p–7:30p	Company class onstage
		8p–11p	Dress/tech run-thru
Tuesday	June 5	5p–7p	Tech preparation
		7p–7:30p	Company class onstage
		8p–11p	Dress rehearsal (video taping)
Wednesday	June 6	5p–7p	Tech preparation
		7p–7:30p	Company class onstage
		8p–11p	Performance #1
Thursday	June 7	6p–7p	Tech preparation
		7p–7:30p	Company class onstage
		8p–11p	Performance #2
Friday	June 8	6p–7p	Tech preparation
		7p–7:30p	Company class onstage
		8p–11p	Performance #3
Saturday	June 9	6p–7p	Tech preparation
		7p–7:30p	Company class onstage
		8p–11p	Performance #4
Sunday	June 10	1p–6p	Technical strike

By the time the technical rehearsal is ready to start, the stage manager and choreographer-director should have a good idea of whether or not it is going to run smoothly. Unfortunately, since theatre time is determined a long time prior to this, the technical rehearsal will have to fit into the predetermined time slot. It is here that a close working relationship between the stage manager and choreographer-director will pay off. Before starting rehearsal, the two should take a few minutes to get together and identify the dances or sections of dances in which they expect to find problems. Then they should outline the amount of time to be spent on each dance, allowing little time for "easy" ones and more time for the "difficult" ones. This is the only way to be assured that the time will not run out before the last dances are set and that there will be enough time for dress rehearsal. Dances can always look better, details can always be improved, but time cannot be expanded. It is tremendously important to the look of the total performance that the director not get buried in detail at the expense of larger concerns. A technical rehearsal may take three hours, all day, or longer, depending on the quality of work in the previous steps (see Sample Worksheet 3.6).

Prior to dress rehearsal, time should be scheduled for the floor to be wet-mopped and dried, about a half hour. Dress rehearsal should take exactly as long as the running time of the show, including intermissions. Some people prefer to run the dress rehearsal on the day of the show; some prefer to run it the day before. Often, because of tightly scheduled theatres, there is no choice. In any event, when the timing of the theatre rehearsal is initially scheduled, it makes some sense to work backward, starting with the date and time of the performance.

Depending on the experience of the dancers and the crew, time can be saved by combining technical and dress rehearsals. Sometimes, professional companies that perform at different theatres every day have only a cue-to-cue rehearsal (see Sample Worksheet 3.7). This method requires a highly skilled crew. Under the best circumstances it is always more than a little spooky to run a show "cold."

Note carefully that in Sample Worksheets 3.6 and 3.7 no time has been set aside for experimenting or for making choreographic or other performance alterations. These timings are for a show that is "ready to go" the minute it arrives in the theatre. However, time for experimentation is another matter. When a new work is being mounted, time for experimentation is extremely important. A good rule of thumb is that experimentation always takes twice as long as

---

SAMPLE WORKSHEET 3.7
Production Schedule: Major Touring Company Dance Concert

Thursday	June 1	9a–1p	Rigging, electrics hang
		1p–2p	Lunch
		2p–6p	Electrics hang, Company equipment load-in
Friday	June 2	8a–12n	Electrics focus, wardrobe preparation
		12n–1p	Lunch
		1p–3p	Company class, spacing, level setting
		3p–5p	Tech work-thru rehearsal
		5p–6p	Tech adjustments
		6p–7p	Dinner
		7p–7:30p	Company class—tech preparation
		7:30p	House open
		8p	Performance
		10p–12m	Company load-out

---

expected. Mounting a fifteen-minute work, depending on complexity, may take ten hours or five days. Rarely does anyone get five days. Experimental time is generally determined by the available time in the theatre weighed against all of the other performance needs.

The schedule for the evening performance will be similar to that of dress rehearsal. Generally, the crew is called at least two hours before performance. The dancers often come three hours early. This allows an hour and a half to do hair and makeup and to organize wardrobe prior to company class. The floor should again be mopped and time should be scheduled for class. This must be coordinated with the stage crew, who many times need the stage to make last-minute adjustments. The timing of all this must be coordinated with the house manager so that the stage is clear and quiet and the main curtain closed prior to the opening of the house. Many companies have a "warm-down" class after the performance. Time for this, sometimes fifteen or thirty minutes, must be scheduled. Crew time must also be scheduled for closing the house for the night. On the day of the last performance, additional crew time must be scheduled to "strike" the show. This is often accomplished by an efficient crew in about two hours.

As is apparent, each step is dependent on the one preceding. If the light plot is not clear or is inappropriate to the theatre, a tremendous amount of time may be lost in the beginning. If the light plot is not followed carefully when the show is being hung, time loss occurs and focusing will begin late. If the dancers lose time spacing, the crew will lose time setting light levels. If both are slow, the cue-to-cue will be late, but if the cue-to-cue is skipped, the technical rehearsal will take longer and be harder on the dancers. And if the ultimate disaster occurs, there will not be time for dress rehearsal. It becomes quickly obvious that lost time has to be made up somewhere and that bad judgment, a disorganized crew, or poor pre-planning can ruin technical theatre rehearsals and exhaust dancers.

If the dancers are not completely prepared when they start the-atre rehearsals, impossible time losses can occur. As a rule, choreog-raphers should not rechoreograph once they are in the theatre. The only time when this rule is not appropriate is when serious problems are caused by the unexpected peculiarities of a particular stage space. Even if a dancer needs to be replaced at the last minute, much of the "fixing" can be done in the studio without tying up the stage, which might be put to better use by the crew. Since the choreogra-pher is a creative artist, this may be one of the most difficult disci-plines to accept; but just as dancers cannot perform well with last minute unrehearsed changes, neither can the technical crew.

CARE AND FEEDING OF DANCERS AND CREW

Stage crews are made up of human beings who work in the the-atre day in and day out. Quite often, especially when in a theatre infrequently, student dancers, professionals, and teachers alike for-get this fact. As they are willing to work all day and all night to pro-duce "one show a year" they expect everyone around them to do the same. It must be remembered that no one on a stage crew would survive very long if expected to work that way on a day-to-day basis. Sometimes crews will refuse to work after the hours scheduled no matter what the disaster. Even if the crew is willing to stay, the director must remember that after scheduled hours salaries gener-ally jump to time-and-a-half, an amount that may not have been planned in the budget. At this point the director may also start pay-ing the performance-quality price of exhausted dancers.

Eating time is another never-to-be-forgotten time factor. The fact that dancers do not eat before a performance has nothing to do with the stage crew; they eat. For some reason unknown to us, hours off for eating are rarely mentioned during the preplanning stage.

Directors who believe that uninterrupted rehearsal time is available may find the crew vanishing for an hour. Consequently, plan on a hungry crew and find out when they go to eat and for how long.

Dancers may be rugged but they, too, need to be protected. The stage manager can do much in this area. Dancers should not be called when they are not needed. It is exhausting and frustrating to sit in a cold theatre for hours watching the crew do its job. If dancers are blinded by a light and cannot retain balance, the lighting design will have to be altered to save the performance. An excellent performance can happen only in an atmosphere in which everyone can perform to the fullest capacity. This requires mutual respect and understanding.

BACKSTAGE PROCEDURES

Dancers should always be aware of the total stage situation. They never should talk to the crew during a performance run. They should not be on-stage when the crew is setting the scenery, rigging pieces, or doing light checks. They should not touch masking pieces or any equipment. Dancers should keep out of the way of technicians and technicians out of the way of dancers, but each must be aware of the others' actions. Adequate time must be scheduled to instruct everyone in safety procedures before starting work on a show. *No one except dancers and crew should be allowed backstage during a performance.* After the performance, dancers should realize that the crew must work in the stage area before going home. This often necessitates a willingness to help move visitors out of the stage area. Many theatres have rules regarding smoking, drinking, and eating backstage. All personnel should be aware of and respect these rules.

WHO IS THE DIRECTOR?

In the studio the choreographer is the director of the rehearsals. Sometimes the choreographer and the artistic director are one and the same person. When there are many choreographers, there is usually an artistic director who heads the entire production. At any rate, the dancers ordinarily know "who the boss is" in the studio. But when they arrive in the theatre, who is the boss?

On one level the technical director of the theatre is the boss, as this person sets the rules of procedure within the theatre and is responsible for the maintenance of equipment and the working conditions of the crew. However, the technical director often does not work a show. Who then, in the day-to-day theatre rehearsals, is the boss? In our opinion the artistic director and the stage manager are the bosses. This is another reason why it is so important that these two people should work well together.

The stage manager is directly responsible for the stage crew and the artistic director is directly responsible for the dancers. Each is responsible to the other. Communications from the dancers to the stage manager should go through the artistic director, just as communications from the stage crew to the artistic director should go through the stage manager. A stage manager cannot function with ten or twenty dancers communicating their likes and dislikes all at once, just as the artistic director cannot concentrate with five or six stage-crew members all chattering about different aspects of the production. The process of channeling communications through the appropriate person can also keep contradictory orders from being given. Mutual respect, understanding, and organization provide the basis for calm, productive working conditions.

4 . Music and Sound

RUBY ABELING   *Concert music director, composer, and accompanist, Department of Dance, California State University, Long Beach.*

ERIC RUSKIN   *Concert music director, composer, and accompanist, Department of Dance, California State University, Long Beach.*

Sometime in the last fifty years, the music associated with modern dance changed dramatically. This is true not only in dance technique classes, but also in performance. Like the "modern" in modern dance, the music created for dances in the period between 1920 and 1950 was a reaction to the "prettiness" and "superficiality" of what had gone before. It was often atonal, angular, irregular, discordant, and surprising. Today, given the two cautions of appropriateness and excellence, nearly any music may be considered a possibility.

SELECTING MUSIC

The process of putting movement and music together can happen in three ways: (1) the choreographer can work with an already composed piece of music; (2) a composer can create a score for an already choreographed dance; (3) a composer and choreographer can develop a piece together, creating a new work simultaneously. Obviously, the best and most satisfying choice of music for a choreographer is a piece done especially for the dance by an excellent and trusted composer. This situation ensures that the music will relate specifically to the dance, have artistic integrity, and minimize copyright problems.

In selecting music for choreography it might be useful to think on two levels. One is what might be thought of as the "nuts and bolts" (tempo, counts, length, etc.) and the other the aesthetics. Both are basic considerations and are, for the most part, specific. Whoever is selecting the music—the choreographer, artistic director, or music director—should ask the following questions about an already composed piece of music:

- Does the length of the music correspond to the length of the dance?
- Does the quality (physicality, energy) of the music relate to the dance in the way you intend?
- Is the proportion or scope of the music appropriate for the dance?
- Is the music already too familiar to the audience from some other exposure or in some other context?

Have someone whose eye and taste you trust look (and listen) with you, bearing these questions in mind.

The fact that you are dealing with an already composed piece of music means that at some time another artist had a vision and invested both time and creative energy to give it form and life. In using this material you should be very careful to preserve the integrity of the work.

In terms of length, there are several ways to make small adjustments. If the music is too short, try having the dance begin in silence and the music enter later. If the discrepancy is not too great, perhaps the dance can end in silence. If the music is much too short, perhaps a series of very short pieces, either by the same or different composers, would solve the problem. If, on the other hand, the music is too long, try having the music start while the curtain is going up. This is a much more difficult problem and the best solution would be to find some other piece of music or have one composed. Occasionally, it works successfully to have the music fade at the end of the dance, but this depends on the choreography and is not always a good choice. It should be used only for artistic reasons, not because of failure to find the proper-length piece of music. Obviously, it is not acceptable to make cuts in a composerís work unless the composer is someone you know who is willing to do it for you.

Whatever your choice of music, remember that your selection will strongly influence what the audience sees. Music that reflects the emotional impact, physical energy, and/or dramatic intent of the dance will reinforce the choreographic statement. Music that for some reason is in contrast with the choreography will deliver an entirely different message.

A few words of warning are in order. The choice of music that is large, powerful, and orchestral may seem exhilarating initially but ultimately may not be satisfying because of the discrepancy between the large number of musicians and the smaller number of dancers.

The choice of music that is already familiar to the audience (from radio, television, video, film, Broadway musicals, etc.) puts you in immediate competition with the original choreography and/or the preconceived ideas the audience has about that music. Be careful that there is artistic intent in your choice of popular music. This music becomes quickly dated and the movement done to it is often much more fun to do than to watch.

The question of copyright is an important consideration. Any score written after 1850 and *anything* on a record, tape, or CD will probably be protected by copyright. This means that the music can be used *only* with the permission of the copyright holder and perhaps the payment of a fee. You must check with the publisher of the score or with the recording company. Their addresses will be printed on the music score or the jacket accompanying the recording. The holder of the copyright may be the composer, heirs, the artists who performed the recording, or their agents. The failure to receive an answer to an inquiry about permission for performance must be considered a "no" answer.

The U.S. Copyright Office has published *A General Guide to the Copyright Act of 1976*. That book plus a number of smaller pamphlets on specific aspects of the law are available at no charge from the Library of Congress, Washington DC 20559. These materials are updated periodically.

PERFORMANCE OF MUSIC

The best, most exciting, and most satisfying choice of music for a dance concert is live. There is a sense of immediacy generated when musicians perform live that cannot be matched by the best professional recording. For the dancers there is the experience of being exposed to the excitement of collaboration, perhaps for the first time.

Including musicians in a dance concert involves a little extra planning. Where will they play? On stage as part of the visual aspect of the dance? In the orchestra pit? In the wings? Will they need microphones (mics)? What about music stands? (Two stands for each musician are helpful to avoid the need for turning pages at awkward places in the music.)

The question of light for musicians is critical. For performing on stage there should be either a special light (placed strategically so that there are no shadows falling on the piano or keyboard or on the score on the stands) or stand lights controlled from the light board. Musicians playing in the pit or the wings will need stand lights, one light for each stand. All decisions about lights should be made with the lighting designer. Blue gel on stand lights will decrease glare for the musicians and help to prevent light from spilling onto the stage or shining into the audience.

The stage manager should control the turning on and off of the mics and lights. Mics may also be needed on stage either for the dancers or performers who will be speaking or to amplify the sound of tap shoes. At the moment, the best mics for this purpose are called Pressure Zone Microphones (PZMs).

TECHNICAL CONSIDERATIONS

The music for a dance concert is best recorded on reel-to-reel tape, although newer formats of DAT (digital audio tape) and recordable CDs (compact discs) are starting to be widely used. Most theatres are now equipped with both DAT and CD players. Reel-to-reel tape is the best format because it can be easily and precisely edited so that when the stage manager calls "Sound" the response can be instantaneous. If an instantaneous cue is not needed and 1 to 1.5 seconds between the "Sound go" cue by the stage manager and the first note of the music is precise enough, pieces can be run from DAT or CD master tapes. The advantage of using DAT and CDs is that these are "digital" recordings, so the hiss and tape noise associated with "analog" reel-to-reel and cassette tape is simply not present.

DAT and CDs are great for storing important music, master copies, and so on because they physically last much longer than analog tapes. Ideally, the best thing to do is to have important music available in all formats: reel-to-reel, cassettes, DAT, and CD. Most local recording studios do not charge much to dub music to other formats. Then you will have provided for all potential needs: performance on any equipment, rehearsal under any circumstances, and short- and long-term storage. But, remember that a dirty cassette cannot be fixed simply by recording to DAT or CD. Sometimes audio filters can be used to eliminate unwanted noise. Ask your local recording studio engineer. In recording sound, as with computers, garbage in, garbage out!

When selecting the tape for your master, buy the best quality you can. This is no place to pinch pennies. High-quality tape not only

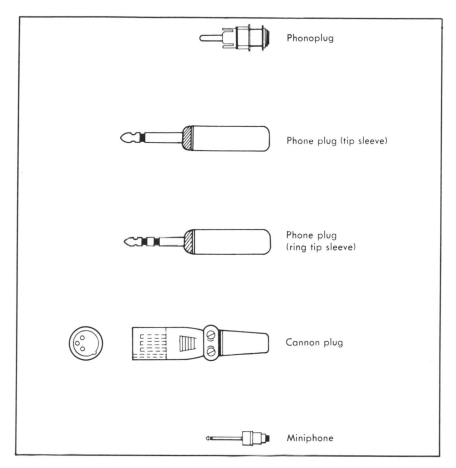

Figure 4.1 Common audio connectors.

will produce cleaner sound (less hiss and background noise) but will also last longer in better condition. When making your tape, go to an expert if you can. Ideally, you want the master tape as free from background noise, clicks, and pops as you can make it. It is also important to have the volume level of recorded sound as high as possible without distortion.

All recording from another source (except live) should be done with cable and plugs (Figure 4.1 shows common audio connectors). Recording with a microphone must be done very carefully, remembering that all people and most things produce unwanted noise. Even things and people outside the room you are in produce audible sounds your recorder may pick up. If you are making a tape of a record, use a *new* tape or record. Old records, even those that have been played only a few times, develop unwanted sounds.

The recording speed 7 1/2 ips (inches per second) is usually safe. Higher numbers (15 ips or 30 ips) will produce better sound, but the tape deck in your performance space may not be able to play back at these speeds. Check first. Another consideration concerns the format of recording and playback: half-track stereo, quarter-track stereo, mono, and so on. Find out the configuration of the tape deck you will be using in performance. Hint: full-track mono will play back successfully on any tape deck. However, it is harder to find and more expensive to purchase a tape recorder that uses this configuration. Professional touring dance companies use this format more frequently because of the variety of sound situations they encounter.

If you tour and your program changes frequently, you will probably find it more useful to keep the music for each of your dances on a separate reel. If all your performances will be the same, it will be simpler to make a master concert tape with the individual pieces strung together, separated by white leader tape, on one or two reels. If you must use two reels, divide the pieces, putting everything before intermission on one reel and everything after intermission on the other. White leader tape is easier to see in a darkened sound booth than other colors because of its contrast with the dark recording tape. Using white leader between pieces makes it easier for the personnel running sound to cue up each piece without problems. Be sure that you always have an exact duplicate of each master tape available as a backup.

The volume of each piece should be checked at rehearsal. Walk around and listen at several different places in the house: down in front, on each side, in the balcony, and especially under the balcony. The goal is to be able to hear clearly and easily without straining and not to feel assaulted by a tremendous amount of sound. You may need to increase sound levels a little in an empty house to allow for acoustical changes caused by an audience. Probably you will also need to have monitor speakers on stage for the dancers. These can be placed downstage and aimed on an upstage diagonal. The volume level for these speakers should be set independently of the house speakers and the sound should not "bleed" into the front rows of seats. The sound operator works from a sound cue sheet (Figure 4.2) set during the technical rehearsal by the music director. The stage manager calls all the sound cues during the running of each piece.

Cue	Description		Stage Monitor	House Front	House Rear	Mixer Pot	Remarks
(1) Stage manager calls beginning.	Two sections of tape —white leader in middle.	MIC UP 22	26	44	30	34	Strike levels at end of piece.
(2) Group runs off stage.							Reset for piece #2.
Stage manager calls beginning.	Tape runs through.	MIC OFF	22	44	28	34	Switch reels for 2nd half of concert.

——INTERMISSION——

Figure 4.2 Sample section of sound cue sheet.

In the large performing space of the theatre, with bigger, more resonant and cleaner sound than in most rehearsal studios and with monitor speakers on stage, the tempo of the music may seem very different to the dancers. This is partly real and partly psychological. There is not a lot that can be done about it except to have the dancers hear it and rehearse to it under these circumstances beforehand. The speeds of various reel-to-reel tape recorders can be somewhat different, but this is unusual. What *is* usual, however, is the greatly varying speeds of the cassette players used for rehearsing.

With a stopwatch, time the master tape being played on the tape recorder you will use in performance. Then time the rehearsal cassette on the cassette player you use for rehearsal. This will indicate if you are going to have a real problem with the tempo of the music, in which case find a cassette player that gives the same total time for your piece as your master tape under performance conditions. This is a guarantee of the same speed.

CARE OF TAPES

Recording tape is a fairly fragile medium. It is very sensitive to variations of temperature and does not survive either extremes of heat (it melts) or cold (it becomes brittle). If it is stretched, the sound recorded on it becomes distorted. If it gets anything on it (oil from hands, smoke, dust) the sound will suffer because the physical condition of the tape has been violated.

No one really knows how long tape will last or how many playbacks it can endure, but the following are some things you can do to ensure as long a life as possible:

1. Store tape at 68 to 70 degrees Fahrenheit, at a relative humidity of about 50 percent.
2. Store tape vertically in airtight canisters. Plastic or metal canisters are best. Horizontal storage is all right for short periods of time.
3. Keep the tapes wound onto the take-up reel and label them "tails out." Every six months or so rewind them all the way onto the playback reel and then back onto the take-up reel at regular playback speed. Do this regularly and you will greatly extend the storage life of your tapes. Tapes you want to preserve should be checked every few years to see if retaping is needed.

4. When playing tapes, allow the tape player to come to a complete stop between functions. Do not subject the tapes to the strain of going from "rewind" to "play," for example, without stopping first.
5. It is an excellent idea to clean the heads of the tape recorder before each use with head cleaning fluid and a Q-tip. In general, avoid sticky fingers, proximity to food, and anything airborne such as smoke, hair spray, or bug spray.

Recording tape is a medium that can be preserved for a fairly long period of time. All it takes is a reasonable amount of cleanliness, care, and common sense.

5 . Costuming*

REGINA FLETCHER SADONO   *Costumer, choreographer, writer, PhD in Theater Arts from the University of California, Los Angeles.*

Dancers use a greater range of movement than do other performing artists, and costumes for dance are an extension of the dancer's movement, never something that is just put on. The dancer's body is the choreographer's medium. For this reason most choreographers will have preconceived ideas about their costumes, and costuming for dance must be a collaboration between the costumer and the choreographer. If you are the choreographer you can skip this step. Otherwise, your first task will be to find out what is in the choreographer's mind, and this can sometimes be a process of showing choreographers what they do not want to see until they know what it is. Be flexible, be prepared to make changes, be patient about getting your ideas across, and be gently persistent when you honestly believe that your idea will enhance the choreographer's vision. Dance costuming is not for the maverick designer with the big, inflexible ego. Costuming for dance must serve the dance, and service is the key concept. Like all costumers, you work diligently behind the scenes, but you will not be in the spotlight and you will not be taking a bow.

GETTING STARTED

If you are doing costumes for dance, it is a good guess that your budget will not be very big. Learning to do things as inexpensively as possible is part of the fun. It is a game that you can win. Before you even start thinking about your design, consider how much money you can spend, and, since you probably will not be getting top dollar for your time, you also need to think ahead about how to economize. Decide what resources are available to you in terms of

*The drawings for this chapter are by Minta Manning.

existing costumes that can be pulled, costume rentals from other schools or studios, thrift stores, and the use of volunteer labor (more on that subject later). If budgets are really tight, you might ask the dancers to contribute old leotards and tights that they no longer use. Most dance costumes are built on leotards, and leotards are expensive—even when you make them yourself. There is no point in starting with a poorly made, ill-fitting leotard any more than there would be in building a house on a shoddy foundation. It also pays to be familiar with catalogue houses, since there are good ones that can make costumes much cheaper than you can. These can be used as they are, or they can be modified to suit your design.

DESIGNING FOR DANCE

First: a little history. Dance reemerged in the West as an art form in the eighteenth century, when humans wore the most cumbersome and restrictive clothing imaginable. Women were squeezed into tight corsets above huge skirts that bulged like mountains at the sides, and men wore ornate high-collared jackets with skirts that jutted out like boats. At the close of the Eighteenth century the French Revolution brought about drastic social changes, deeply affecting the way people thought about themselves and also the way they dressed. Democracy as it existed in ancient Greece became the ideal for human government, and it also became fashionable to imitate classical Greek art, Greek theatre, Greek sculpture, Greek architecture, and Greek lines in clothing. This, as can be imagined, brought about a revolution in artistic dance, as it freed the naturally beautiful lines of the human body and, even more importantly, freed the body to move. Not long afterward (in 1832) Marie Taglioni appeared in *La Sylphide* wearing a costume that gave the illusion that she was floating in a cloud. This became the prototype for the Romantic tutu, and as dance continued to evolve into an ever greater range of athleticism, more and more of the body was revealed. Hemlines grew shorter until finally the entire leg was exposed and the pelvic area framed in a tiny, symbolic skirt.

By the beginning of the twentieth century, the dancer in her hip length tutu was a familiar sight, and ballet, which had become somewhat stagnant, had a rebirth with the creative innovations of the Ballets Russes. The work of modern dance pioneers, such as Loie Fuller and Isadora Duncan, put another spin on what the well-dressed dancer wore, and costuming extended the dancer's space. The general trend over time has been to streamline, and unless the costume is being used specifically as a distortion it now conforms to the curves and the shape of the body as much as possible.

Although modern dance continually developed new ideas, the marriage between ballet and the tutu remained pretty much intact until the collaboration between the Russian designer Karinska and the choreographer George Balanchine opened up new possibilities. "When . . . Balanchine was asked by the Ford Foundation in 1963 what he most needed for his work, he answered with one word: 'Karinska!'" (Toni Bentley, *Costumes by Karinska*, p. 8). Chapter 5 of *Costumes by Karinska* contains invaluable insights into dance costuming for both men and women. Karinska was very sensitive to the needs of the dancer and found ways to meld the tutu both with the dancer's body and with Balanchine's creative ideal. She insisted that her costumes look beautiful from the inside as well, since what the dancer steps into before she goes on stage will affect how she feels about herself and will impact on her performance. Karinska also tried to use natural fabrics as much as possible, since these move and breathe more freely with the dancer. (More on choosing fabrics later.)

THE DESIGN PROCESS

Color

If you do not already have a little book of colors, go out and buy one, since this will be the quickest way for you and your choreographer to agree. You can never underestimate the importance and the impact of color. Since many dance costumes are minimal, color can be the area of greatest exploration.

- Learn the basics. Read *Color Me Beautiful,* by Carole Jackson, and learn which colors go with which skin types. Work this into your overall concept if possible.
- Think of contrasts. Try putting colors together that no one else has thought of; see how it looks.
- Get some ideas and put a palette together just from your sense of what the piece is about.
- Remember that colors change drastically under theatre lighting, white most of all. Flat colors make the dancer look flat, and muted or blended colors can give the piece a textured, sculpted look.
- If you decide to dye, you might want to experiment with some tie-dye effects. (More on dyeing later.)

MEASUREMENT CHART

Dancer _____

Telephone _____ Dance(s) _____

Address _____ _____

_____ _____

Height _____ Weight _____ Bust (chest) _____

Waist _____ Hip _____ Neck _____

Shoulder seam _____ Shoulders (back) _____

Center back to waist _____

Upper arm (elbow raised and bent) _____ Lower arm _____

Armscye to waist _____ Waist to knee _____

To floor over hip _____ Neck to floor _____

Trouser inseam _____ Thigh _____ Calf _____

Ankle _____ Hat size _____ Brow_____

Hairline to base of skull _____ Ear to ear (over head) _____

Hair color _____ Style_____

Street clothing:

Shirt _____ Pants _____ Dress _____

Blouse _____ Shoe _____

Dance clothing:

Tights _____ Leotard _____ Ballet shoes _____

Miscellaneous:

Figure 5.1 Sample measurement chart.

- A layering of colors that are revealed as the dancer moves is extremely effective.

Scheduling

When you have a collection of samples for the choreographer to choose from or reject, set up a preliminary meeting that will include watching the early stages of rehearsal and some extra time to take measurements. A measuring chart (Figure 5.1) should include more measurements than you need, since it is hard in tight production schedules to go back for seconds. Whenever possible, do the measurements yourself rather than getting them over the phone from the dancer. It is amazing how many different ways there are to read a tape measure!

- Sit down with the choreographer and find out what the dance is about.
- Find out about the music.
- Find out what kind of lighting will be used. Some performances are done outside during the day and this will affect the kind of choices the costumer makes.
- Decide how much creative license you have and how much of your work will be helping the choreographer actualize what he or she has in mind. (Figure 5.2)
- Go over your color samples and talk about fabrics.
- Go over the production schedule and nail down those deadlines.
- Find out what comes before and after your dance so that you know how much time the dancers will have for a costume change.

Remember that unless your costumes are leotards or unitards, the dancers will need time to work in them, so get them done well before the dress rehearsal. Handling a skirt in a dance with a lot of falls and rolls takes practice, especially for beginners. If you cannot get your costumes done that soon, find equivalent rehearsal clothes. If you are making tutus, carefully consider the effects of partnering. Schedule time for the dancer to work in the costume to make sure that she and her partner can move comfortably.

Fabrics

When you go to the fabric store introduce yourself to the clerk, and mention that you are a costumer in a way that lets her know you are a professional who is going to bring them business. After you have selected some fabrics based on the way they move when you wave them around, go back to the clerk and ask her to cut some swatches. Most fabric stores are used to this, especially in larger cities, and some of them will even allow you to cut the swatches yourself. If they are resistant, just give a look of sympathy because of all the business they will lose and ask them to recommend another store. That should do the trick.

"Inscape"
Choreography: Bella Lewitzky, 1976
Music: Larry Attaway
Decor/Costume: Rudi Gernreich

Lighting design: Darlene Neel
Technical design: Newell Taylor Reynolds
Dancer: Claudia Schneiderman

Vic Luke

Figure 5.2 As a dancer, Rudi Gernreich began designing costumes for the Lester Horton Company in the 1940's. From a renowned career in public fashion, he returned to dance to design "Inscape" for Bella Lewitzky. "Inscape" is a danced panorama of fleeting illusions and allusions which refer the viewer to societal attitudes and invite multiple responses. Lewitzky and Gernreich conceived of both dance and decor as having equal validity, function, and purpose.

Since dance is about movement, the way that the fabric moves is of the utmost importance. Natural fabrics usually move the best. You know what the dance is about, you have heard the music, so you will know whether to choose a fabric that is heavy or light. If you want something that flows around the body like water, choose silk. It is expensive, but it moves like nothing on earth and is worth the extra expense to be able to accentuate the dancer's movement in this way. Keep your eyes peeled for sales and become familiar with some mail-order houses that offer good bargains. Aside from its exquisite relationship with gravity, silk comes in many weights and textures and takes dye beautifully. Some basic costuming concepts:

Unitard
Leotard with tights
Leotard with skirt
Leotard with loose-fitting
   pants
Loose-fitting pants with shirt
Street wear or everyday clothes
Leotard designed to suggest
   street clothes
Ethnic or religious costumes
Classic dance dress (fitted bodice
   and gored skirt)
Evening clothes
Masks or other built-on shapes
Technological and/or multi-
   media links

Uniforms suggestive of an
   occupation
Totally creative clothing designs
Period costumes
Costumes for classical ballet
Costumes for vaudeville or
   theatrical dance
Clothing suggestive of a sport or
   luxury activity
Costumes based on mythical
   creatures
Costumes imitating or suggesting
   animals
A combination of two or more or
   these

(Remember shoes, headwear, and accessories)

Chances are your idea will fit loosely into one of these categories. At this point you will want to prepare renderings to bring to the choreographer. If you do not draw well, get some tracing paper and a book about dancers or dance technique that has some good photographs. Trace a body, then sketch your design over the tracing. This will at least communicate your basic idea and will get you and the choreographer thinking along the same lines. If you are going to use street clothes for your design, go to a second-hand store and pick out an item or two that will represent your ideas.

MAKING IT WORK

Unitards are becoming the most commonly used costume, unfortunately, since they are monotonous and do no real justice to most bodies. However, they can be dyed and/or cut in many different ways to make them more interesting. Next in popularity (for women) are leotards with skirts (Figure 5.3). These are relatively easy to make and offer different "looks" with a changed hemline, neckline, or draped effect. They can also be enhanced with hats, shoes, belts, and assorted accessories.

"Suite Satie"
Choreography: Bella Lewitzky, 1980
Music: Erik Satie

Decor and lighting design: Darlene Neel
Dancers: Claudia Schneiderman, Serina
Richardson, Amy Ernst

Dan Esgro

Figure 5.3 The lyric dancing of "Suite Satie" is enhanced by flowing sheer skirts with individualized leotards.

Skirts

To create a circle skirt on a leotard, put the leotard on the dancer after it has been dyed and draw a pencil line from the protrusion of the hip bone curving down to just above the navel in the front, gently over the opposite hip and dipping down to the center of the lower back (Figure 5.4).

Cut out a full circle skirt, in two halves to save fabric (Figure 5.5). You can easily create a pattern for yourself with newspaper, a pencil, and a string. Use the hip measurement to estimate the waistline, better too small than too large if you are not sure. Finish the waistline of the skirt on an overlock machine and make pencil marks at even intervals on the waistband of the skirt and on the leotard, to match up when you pin. (Figures 5.6 a and b.) Then pin the skirt to the leotard at the sides and at the center front and back. Then add four more pins at half points between those and stretch the leotard gently to fit as you sew the skirt in place. (It is easier to do this on the dancer, but if you cannot, try stretching the leotard

Figure 5.4 Sample of a finished skirt applied to a leotard. Note how the top line follows the wearer's hipline.

over an ironing board.) A smooth waistline will be the most flattering, but there can also be some gathering at the waist for a fuller effect. The skirt can also be made with a closure in the back, and it can be made with one and a quarter or one and a half circles for a really flowing look. It can be made as a separate garment to be worn over the leotard or unitard.

For a different look, the skirt can be sewn on higher up, above the waist or under the bustline (Figure 5.7). Be sure the finished effect is smooth, since any protrusions from the body interrupt the lines and should be avoided unless they are intentional.

Remember that if you use silk, part of the circle will be cut on the bias of the fabric (see glossary), and this part will stretch longer at the hem. It is best to let the skirt hang for several days before you attempt the final cut. To make your life easier, schedule a time to finish the hem while the skirt is on the dancer. Mark a yardstick at the distance of the hem from the floor and have the dancer turn in place while you make pencil marks on the skirt where you want the length. A helper comes in handy to hold the yardstick while you make the marks. Then lay the skirt down and cut along the circle that is suggested by the marks. Generally, with decent silk, you can leave a raw edge on the hem. If you decide to finish the hem on the overlock, you may need to repeat the operation later, when the silk stretches again. There are also hem sealers, but these are messy and leave a dark

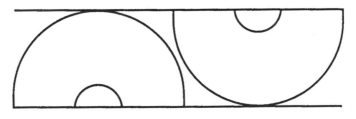

Figure 5.5 Placement of pattern for circle skirt.

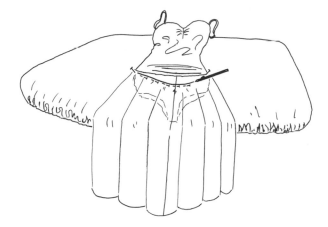

Figure 5.6a A leotard can be stretched to a dancer's hip measurement and pinned to an ironing board. The skirt can then be applied and the style line marked.

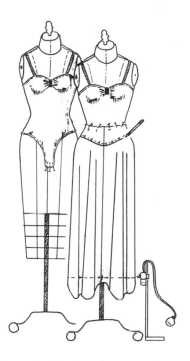

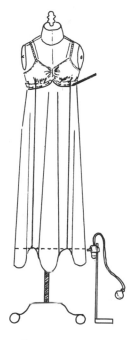

Figure 5.6b Another method of marking the application of a full-circle skirt onto a leotard using a dress form without legs.

Figure 5.7 Sample of a three-quarter-circle skirt being draped on a leotard.

Figure 5.8 Bodice pattern with side-front panel cut on bias.

edge along the hem line. The skirt can also be attached to a bodice, for a more classical look (Figure 5.8). Add silk chiffon, net, or tulle for more lightness; heavier fabric gives a period look or one more suggestive of everyday clothes.

Standard patterns

In general, pattern books are a good resource, since a ready-made clothing pattern can be used as a basis for your design. A good pattern for drawstring pants is very useful. For most clothing patterns it is easy to add a gusset at the crotch and/or armhole to enhance the movement range (Figure 5.9). Make a mark on your pattern about four inches down from the armpit or crotch in-seam. Lay

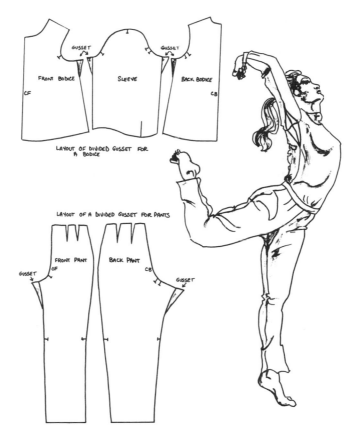

Figure 5.9 Underarm and crotch seam gusset.

the pattern on a piece of paper and draw a line that extends the seam line gradually outward to about two inches from the crotch or armhole line. For sleeves this procedure should be repeated on the sleeve part of the pattern, so that the two holes will match in size.

If you are handed a drawing and are really lost about how to begin to turn it into something to wear, chances are there is a pattern that can at least get you through step one. There are also many books and classes on patternmaking, if you want to develop your skills in that area. Also remember that you can take any garment (including a leotard) apart at the seams, and make a pattern out of it. As a general rule you make a pattern smaller or larger by cutting it in quarters and either overlapping it or spreading it out. Trace the old pattern piece onto a new piece of paper, and cut the new piece roughly into quarters (halves if you only need to adjust length). Lay down your quarters either spread out or overlapped, and draw the new pattern onto another piece of paper in the required size.

TUTU CONSTRUCTION

Making a tutu from scratch is a painful ordeal; unless you are an experienced, dedicated, and inspired seamstress with lots of patience, use a good resource that makes professional-looking tutus in a range of sizes, colors, and styles. Plan on giving at least several months' notice on the order, especially in the autumn. If you would like to build a tutu, you will discover that it is hard to find a pattern because costuming has traditionally been a closed shop and costumers tend to keep their secrets.

Before you start, read Chapter 5 of Toni Bentley's book *Costumes by Karinska*. Karinska deserves credit for many creative innovations in tutu construction, such as cutting the side-front bodice panel on the bias of the fabric for increased fit and flexibility (see Figure 5.8). She also modernized the tutu in many respects, creating sweeping effects with a few layers of tulle on a simple bodice for Balanchine's *Serenade*. There is also some good information in the Karinska biography on placing jacket sleeves for male dancers so that the jacket stays in place and does not bunch up at the shoulders when they lift their arms.

The following instructions are not guaranteed, since it takes skill, ingenuity, and experience to go from words to a finished product. Do not even try if you do not have a tutu to study. It is even better if you can find an old tutu to take apart. If so, take notes on all the construction elements that you observe along the way. If it is a well-constructed tutu, you can make a pattern from it. The standard tutu consists of three parts, a panty, a yoke that extends from the waist to the hip bones, and a bodice that is sewn over the yoke.

Tutu panties

To get a pattern for panties, buy an inexpensive pair of plain cotton underwear of the size that your dancer will wear. Cut across the middle of the crotch panel and then down the center of the back. Open them out and lay them flat, and you will see the shape of the piece that you will be working with (Figure 5.10). Then cut it in half down the front center seam and lay one half over your pattern paper.

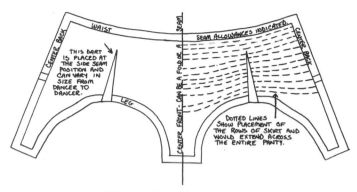

Figure 5.10 Tutu: panty.

Trace around the edges, leaving a seam allowance all around. Take the resulting pattern and place it with the front center seam at the edge of some "girdle fabric." (It stretches and has the same stiffness as a girdle. Not all fabric stores carry it.) Cut two pieces and join at the front center seam. After this, fit the dancer and mark the panty at the protrusions of her hip bones. This is the place where the yoke will eventually be sewn over the panty, and will mark the top layer of net or tulle. Once the panty has been fitted—sometimes including a small dart at the sides—use a pencil to extend the marks at the hip bones into a line that goes all around the panty, parallel to the top edge.

Based on what kind of a tutu you want, you will decide how many layers of net or tulle to sew on. You might want a compact tutu with a large circumference. You can create different effects with the length and stiffness of the fabric. A short classical tutu is made with net, alternating every third layer with stiff net, to about twelve rows (less for small dancers, more for tall ones). Each layer is one inch shorter than the one above, so start with thirteen inches for the top row on a twelve-layered tutu, and work down to a row that is two inches (approximately an inch is turned under in the process of attachment).

Mark all the lines on the panty before you begin, which involves a little arithmetic, based on the size of your dancer. You have to fit twelve lines between the top line and one and one half inches from the bottom edge. Once you start doing this, notice that the lines get closer together over the top of the leg and farther apart across the front and back of the panty where there is more space. Practice a few times on a piece of scratch paper until you get the hang of it. For a Romantic tutu, you will need only five or six layers of tulle, but the same formula applies, with the layers sewn as closely together as possible.

When you are ready to cut the net or tulle, get some help. Use a cutting board or mark the lengths on a work-bench before you begin. Cutting across the grain of the fabric, each row will take approximately four lengths of fabric (3.5 for a Romantic tutu), so cut four at thirteen inches, four at twelve inches, and so on until you have all your rows. *Label them.* Go through the same process for a Romantic tutu, but base the hem length on the dancer's size.

Once all the fabric is cut, sew the lengths together into one long row, leaving it open at both ends, then put a gathering thread along the top edge. This takes time and uses lots of thread. (Use good-quality thread to avoid breakage.) Once you have completed this, sew on the top layer first. Gather the fabric so that it fits along the top line on the panties, then pin it in place with the raw edge toward the bottom. Be sure to leave room at the back edge so that there is enough fabric to fold over and make a closure. This process takes time; do not rush. Play soothing music. Breathe deeply. Have your favorite radio program or television talk show going on in the background.

When the fabric is pinned in place, machine-sew it down with a zigzag stitch. Keep going until you get all the layers on, and be prepared to feel a little cramped toward the end. (It helps to pin the rows above out of the way with big safety pins before going on to the next.) When you are finished, make a casing at the leg of the panty for an elastic. Sew over one inch (for a half-inch elastic) with the hem toward the inside of the garment. Put the elastic in the casings and fit the skirt on the dancer. Notice at this point that the skirt is just one big ball of net. The layers will have to be tacked together to compact the skirt, which should be done when the entire garment is complete. (See below for instructions on how to tack.)

You will be finished at this point if you want a plain-looking tutu, but you may want to add an overskirt for trim. You can also sew trim directly onto the net. Use a light fabric for the overskirt, or match the fabric of the bodice. Cut a circle that fits over the top layer of net, keeping an opening at the back. Finish the hem as needed, leaving a few inches of net showing, and baste the skirt in place before you sew on the yoke.

Tutu yoke

The next step is to make the yoke (Figure 5.11). Use a pattern for a straight skirt that is about the same size as your dancer. Trace over

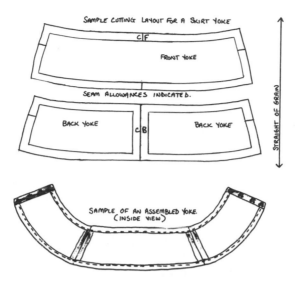

Figure 5.11 Tutu: yoke.

it to make a yoke that extends from her waist to the top of her hip bones. This should be made from the same sturdy fabric as the bodice and, like the bodice, it should be lined with iron-on facing, then lined again with a softer fabric. You can make the lining separately or join it to the yoke with an overlock stitch all around each separate piece. This will give a finished edge on the seams and make a sturdy garment. Before you make the closure at the back, sew a length of sturdy bias tape along the inside of the waistband. This will help to hold the skirt in place while the dancer moves. The finished yoke will be fitted to the dancer with an opening at the back that coincides with the back opening of the bodice. The yoke is then sewn over the panty, folding over a hem and just catching the top of the overskirt or the top row of net.

You might skip this step and make a longer bodice for a different look, but the yoked garment will be easier to fit and easier to dance in. Once it is attached to the skirt, fit the skirt on the dancer. Gather up the elastics and sew the crotch together at the center. Put the skirt on the dancer again and fit the back closure. Use hook-and-eye tape for the closure on the panty, since it does not show. If you can, find "bar"-type eyes rather than loops. These are preferable because they hold the tutu closer to the body. You will need a large hook and eye for the waist, and then sew on the others as indicated for the best fit.

Tutu bodice

Bodices (see Figure 5.8) can be tricky, so it is important to have a good pattern and to schedule many fittings. Trial and error is the way to learn this. If you do not have a bodice pattern, go to the fabric store and look through the pattern books. Many clothing patterns, for example, for wedding and evening dresses, use bodices in their construction, and with some ingenuity these can be modified to suit your needs.

Start with a mock-up and fit it on the dancer to refine your ideas. Put the mock-up on the dancer inside out and pin to fit. Make pencil marks where the pins are before you remove them. Then use the pencil lines to set your seams or darts. After you have worked with your mock-up and feel confident that you know what you are doing, cut out the bodice. Before you sew the panels together, line them with iron-on facing. Cut a second bodice out of lining fabric. Put all three layers together and stitch around each piece with an overlock, as you did with the yoke. Then sew the front center seam, and work your way along to the side-back panels. Fit the garment on the dancer and make whatever adjustments are necessary, then fold over the back closure seams as indicated by the fitting. The garment should be boned at the side front seams with boning that extends just to the bottom of the rib cage. Fit the bodice again. The dancer should not be wearing anything at this final fitting that she will not be wearing under her costume on stage.

The bodice needs to be snug, but remember, the dancer needs to breathe. To prevent gaping, sew on an elastic that extends from an inch in front of the side seam, along the upper edge of the bodice, down to one inch away from the back closure. You can sew the elastic straight to the bodice with a zigzag stitch or place a casing so that you can draw up the elastic to fit. Put the bodice on the dancer one more time and mark the closure for the back. Make the closure with hooks and eyes, using a large sturdy hook at the top.

Sew shoulder elastics at the front and measure the bodice on the dancer before sewing them in place at the back. Elastics should be tight but not restrictive. It is a good idea to trim the bodice before you sew it to the skirt. Designing the trim is an enjoyable part of the creative process, so take plenty of time in the fabric store and play. The trim should be placed so that it enhances the flattering V-shape of the bodice front. Reflect your bodice trim in the overskirt.

Tutu finishing

Once both the bodice and skirt are complete, they must be joined. Put both of them on the dancer and pull the center of the "point" of the bodice to the center of the yoke. Pin in place and then pin at the side seams. Place two more pins at midpoints on the front and two at the back, then remove the tutu and mark your pin placements. Make sure that the bodice lays flat along the yoke, repinning if necessary, then baste in place. After a final fitting, sew on by hand with sturdy buttonhole thread, or by machine. Leave the very point of the bodice free for those deep backbends. Fit the tutu on the dancer one more time to check the closure and then sew on the hooks and eyes.

If you do not have experience with tacking, do it first while the dancer wears the costume. Notice that the top layer of the skirt should be horizontal to the floor and that the other layers need to be drawn up gently for support. The process involves the biggest, longest needle that you can find and thread the same color as the skirt.

Knot a double thread and start underneath the skirt, next to the back opening and catching in the smallest layer of net. Draw the needle up through all the layers so that the result is compact but not tight. Move the needle about two inches along a line that circles the garment about an inch from where the skirt is attached to the yoke. Send the needle back through the layers, catching in the bottom row. Again draw up the thread so that the layers are compact but not tight. Continue in the same way all around the circle until you get to the back closure on the other side. Then start a second circle about an inch farther out, and continue around as before. Repeat this, moving gradually toward the outer rim, until you have made as many circles as you need to compact the entire skirt. Be careful that you pay attention to what is happening to the net at the back. This part of the skirt will be pulled together by the closure of the garment, and if these ends are not neatly sewn in, you will end up with a kind of "duck-tail effect" that is not very nice. Some seamstresses do the tacking in "spokes" starting from the center and working out to the hem, instead of in concentric circles. Either way is fine.

To store the finished garment, hang it upside down from the panty on a skirt hanger, being careful that the bodice hangs free. This prevents gravity or closet crowding from making the tutu droop. Romantic tutus should also be hung this way, since these skirts can also lose their buoyancy. Most tutus can be washed by hand, carefully, and allowed to dry upside down. Only specialty dry cleaners, who advertise that they clean costumes, will handle a garment with a lot of trim.

DYE AND COLOR TREATING

Materials and supplies for dyeing

- Large noncorrosive receptacle: aluminum, stainless steel, porcelain, or enamel (Do not use cookware, since most dye is *toxic*)
- Salt to prevent the dye from fading and running
- Bleach to remove dye mistakes
- Rubber gloves
- Dye pigment
- Stir stick
- Water softener
- A heating source, such as a stove or hot plate (not necessary for all fabrics)
- Color remover (optional but necessary for fabrics like nylon)
- A well-ventilated work area for working with toxic substances
- Miscellaneous: smaller pots and containers for mixing and testing, nylon stocking for straining
- Rubber bands or string (for tie-dye)

If you plan to dye swatches and need to match colors, set up an iron and ironing board covered with a towel. After you dye your swatch, place it on the towel and iron dry to get a true color. Wet fabric is several shades darker than dry. You will need a way to dispose of your dye waste that will not kill plants or fish.

Instructions

1. Prepare fabric by washing, do not dry. Avoid extreme temperature changes, which cause shrinkage.
2. Read instructions on the dye package, then mix dye completely in small container to a pastelike consistency.
3. Add salt, about 1 teaspoon salt to 1 teaspoon dye pigment, to reduce fading.
4. Strain mixture through a nylon stocking or cheesecloth.

5. Water in receptacle should be soft and the dye added gradually while the mixture is stirred.

6. Test color with a swatch of fabric intended to be dyed. (If you order leotards for dyeing ask the company to send you a few scraps of material that can be used to test colors.) Record the amount of dye used and also the time the swatch was kept in the dye bath in order to duplicate the color at need.

7. Fabric should be wet, unfolded, and untwisted when dropped into the dye bath for an even coloration. Remember that all fabric should be prewashed whenever possible to account for any shrinkage and to get rid of dirt or chemical pretreatments before the dye is added. Once the fabric is prepared, it should be dropped into the dye bath quickly. If you want an uneven look, drop the fabric in unevenly. Use string or rubber bands for a tie-dye effect (see below). You can also dip dye: sleeves in one bath, body in another; progressively lighter colors moving up toward the waist of a skirt.

8. Stir continually. If unwanted spotting occurs, it may be because you did not stir dye solution, because the temperature was too low, or because you did not allow the fabric to remain in the dye bath long enough.

9. Remove and rinse thoroughly with cold water.

10. Remember that most fabric can be dyed in the washing machine and this is a good option when there is a large quantity to be dyed. You can swatch test when the washer is full, then drop in your fabric and continue the cycle once you have established the right amount. After using the washing machine to dye, run another cycle (or two) empty with soap and a cup of bleach to clean out the tub.

A few notes on tie-dye. Rubber bands work better than string. This is a creative process, so practice with a few T-shirts first to get some ideas. Prepare the garment for dyeing and place the rubber bands or string around gathered parts of the wet costume, where you want to prevent the fabric from soaking up the dye, before placing it in the dye bath. To get a two-tone effect, dye with the fabric tied, then take out the bands and drop the fabric into a lighter color. You can also dip dye up to the rubber band in one color, rinse, then turn the garment upside down and dip dye up to the rubber band with another color. Use your imagination!

Dye can also be painted on, spattered on, dusted on (in dry form), dripped on, sprayed on, bleached out, or batiked. Remember that many of these techniques will leave a costume that will have to be hand-washed separately in cold water or dry-cleaned. For painting on fabric, acrylic and latex paints are best since they are flexible when they dry and hold up in the washing machine. You need to apply the paint and allow it to dry with the dancer in the costume (this takes about an hour). Other techniques for putting color on fabric include appliqué, spray paint, marker pens, and various kinds of trim. Dye can be prepared and applied with a spray bottle; lay costume flat or hang upright to create different effects.

A FEW LAST THOUGHTS

About computers

What can computers do for the average dance costumer? Not much. Most of the software that is out there is aimed at the big design studios and is probably way out of your reach. Unless you are affiliated with a university that has a state-of-the-art computer room, you probably will not find a computer that will have much to offer. There are some applications to costuming, though, if you have access to a word processor, graphics software, and/or a spread sheet. A computer can be very helpful for keeping track of inventory, measurements, calendars, deadlines, phone numbers, and things-to-do, and simple graphics software can produce a top-notch flyer and/or a very professional-looking invoice for billing. If you do have access to an up-to-date computer room, fabrics can be scanned into a computer to embellish your designs, and those technophiles with limited drawing skills might find computer graphics useful.

About helpers

Costumers are often in a position to recruit volunteer labor, especially if they are working for a studio or a school for young people. This may be the only possible way to get the job done. Mothers will be willing, but it will be rare to find one who isn't working for her own child rather than for the production as a whole. Also, most people usually agree to more than they can do, so give them less than they want to take. It's also important to establish the line of command at the beginning, so get the choreographer to work with you on this.

Backstage

When your costumes are ready to go into the theater, bring hangers and find out what storage facilities the theater can provide. Be prepared to do a little "in-service training" with your dancers, especially if they are beginners, since they may need to be taught how to pick up a garment, place it on a hanger, and then place the hanger on a rack. (Really!) Dancers *must know* that this is their responsibility. The way they treat their costume is just as important as what they do on stage. No food in the costume room. No eating in costume. No costumes in the house, unless it is a planned public relations event. Get the choreographer to help you with this. Costumes have to be labeled, so get an indelible marking pen and either use an existing label or sew one in. Find out what will happen to the costumes after the show. Who will wash them? Where will they be stored? Who will do the after show inventory to make sure that nothing walks away or gets left behind? For a big show, an inventory sheet is a must. Delegate responsibility, wisely.

About dancers

Dancers are subject to a rigid and unnatural aesthetic that does much to aggravate the already complex and negative attitude that women develop about their physique. To see how far this can go, read Gelsey Kirkland's autobiography, *Dancing On My Grave.*

The male dancer is under just as much pressure to conform to a rigid aesthetic and he is also prone to have negative attitudes about his body that will emerge in all kinds of complaints as soon as he puts on his costume. All too often the costumer becomes the scapegoat for the dancers' (and/or the choreographer's) dissatisfaction with themselves and their bodies as well as an outlet for the frustrations, insecurities, and miscellaneous fears of failure that are associated with performing arts production. These situations require a sophisticated handling of temperaments, both theirs and your own. Be a good listener, and do not take things personally. Your costumes are an expression of you, but as soon as the dancer wears them they are an expression of him or her. Unlike a painting that hangs on a wall or a book that you buy in a store, a costume is never a finished product until the dancer "owns" it. On the other hand, a costumer should never relinquish artistic control. It is a matter of diplomacy, and the closer you are to production, the more diplomacy you will need. Best of luck!

SOURCES

- Discount Dance Supply, PO Box 8068, Laguna Hills, CA 92654. Phone 800-328-7107 www.discdance.com. Good catalogue, reasonable prices, and they are fast.
- Primadonna Tutus, 2 Penn Center Plaza #200, Philadelphia, PA 19102-1706. Phone: 215-236-3707.
- Rupert, Gibbon & Spider, PO Box 425, Healdsburg, CA 95448. Phone: 800-442-0455. An excellent mail-order resource for silk. They have a wide variety of stock at a reasonable price.
- Theatre Development Fund Costume Collection, 601 West 26th Street, New York, NY 10001. Phone: 212-989-5855. Rents costumes to nonprofit organizations, and has developed an on-line tutu registry.

6 . Lighting

DORIS EINSTEIN SIEGEL   *Lighting designer. Professor Emeritus, Department of Dance, University of California, Los Angeles.*

Stage lighting is a very specialized field. Stage lighting for the dance is one of its rarefied subspecialties. Both are a mixture of practical, technical know-how and black magic. If uninitiated persons listen in on a lighting rehearsal, the language will leave them convinced that it is all in secret code. They can listen for hours and have no idea what actually transpires. All they can see are the final results.

Perhaps that is as it should be. The choreographer can experiment in the privacy of the studio. A composer can work out musical ideas alone or with other musicians. A designer of costumes and scenery can develop sketches on a drawing board. The lighting designer's images can be realized only very publicly, usually under great economic pressure involving time, space, and personnel.

As light does have magic qualities, the temptation for onlookers to try to get "into the act" is often irresistible. To protect themselves from "help" that very often will interfere with a basic creative process, lighting designers have three choices: to be deaf, to be rude, or to speak in mumbo jumbo, comprehensible only to the initiated and therefore potentially truly helpful. And that, I am convinced, is how the language of stage lighting was born.

PURPOSES OF LIGHTING

Unquestionably, the main purpose of lighting is to make a dance visible. A performance in bright daylight, indoors or out, requires little or no additional illumination. Yet even under these circumstances we may be aware that the nature of light adds a new dimension to the performance. Perhaps some parts of the area are lighter than others. Perhaps there is a bright ray of sunshine cutting through a tree or coming through a window. Some dancers may be moving and facing toward the source of light, others away from it. These conditions may be random "happenings" in the dance or they may be used by the choreographer to dramatic advantage.

In a theatre environment, where random light can be eliminated, complete control of light rests with the lighting designer. Regardless of the size of the theatre or the degree of experience and professionalism of the company, the aims and the process of lighting design remain the same. Everything that occurs should happen with a purpose. Lighting must illuminate, providing both vision and insight. It can externalize the mood of the work, define the space, build an environment, emphasize selected elements, clarify relationships, enhance the three-dimensionality of the space and the performers, give a sense of focus, and direct the viewers' attention. Its flow can convey the continuity or fragmentation of the action within the dance.

Mood

Lighting often establishes the mood of a work, sometimes before any dancer enters the stage. The environment on the stage can be made to "feel" happy or sad, romantic or stark, and can be given a sense of spaciousness or enclosure. The use of color is a primary element in creating mood. It appears that some colors evoke a fairly universal emotional reaction, whereas others are more ambiguous. The sun-and-fire related "warm" colors tend to suggest action, happiness, or passion; the sky-water-and-forest related "cool" colors may suggest repose, contemplation, and possibly sadness.

The intensity of light affects our feelings or mood. We tend to associate brightness with high spirits, dimness with depression. The direction of the light may affect the viewer, with vertical beams giving a sense of aspiration and horizontal ones a sense of being earthbound (Figure 6.1).

These examples may appear somewhat simplistic. They are meant merely to suggest elements of a vocabulary that each designer of lighting will arrive at individually. Usually, through associations and past experiences, an audience will perceive what the designer wants to convey.

Space

In many theatrical productions, space is defined by the use of scenery. Dance theatre tends to use scenery sparingly, mostly for aesthetic, but at times for economic, reasons. Scenery is expensive. Scenery may take up space, and dance productions jealously guard

"Missa Brevis"　　　　　　　　　　Scenic design: Malcolm McCormick
UCLA Dance Company　　　　　　　Lighting design: Doris Siegel
Choreography: José Limón

Marcia Roltner

Figure 6.1 Light may give a sense of aspiration and highlight movement to which special attention is to be drawn.

space for use by the dancers. Lighting can build an environment independent of props and scenery. At one and the same time, it creates space and saves space. Space defined by light does not interfere with the movement of the performers and is infinitely flexible.

Does the dance occupy the full stage or is the movement confined to a small, intimate area? Is the movement low, pressed to the ground or does it soar to heights? Does some action occur in one place only to be repeated at a later time in another place? Does action take place simultaneously in two or more unconnected places? Are these alike? Do they differ? Is the movement confined to a path? A plane? Is some part of the space more important than another? Do we want a dancer to "disappear" without exiting from the stage?

By careful choice and location of lighting instruments, the shaping of their beams and their relative intensities, a designer can define these and many other spatial concepts. The use of projected images on either the background or the floor can do much to give a

"Events and Reverberations"   Costume design: Malcolm McCormick
UCLA Dance Company   Lighting design: Doris Siegel
Choreography: Carol Scothorn

Marcia Roltner

Figure 6.2 Light can clarify the relationships among the dancers. A special light on a dancer may differentiate her in character from other performers.

sense of design and often add to the mood and atmosphere of the stage picture.

Relationships

Lighting can do much to clarify the relationship among the dancers on the stage (Figure 6.2). It can indicate that all dancers are together or in separate unconnected groups or worlds. A difference in the color used on dancers may help to indicate differences in strength, intensity, or character. A special light on one or more dancers, different in quality or color, can point up a breaking away from the rest of the action on the stage. What lighting cannot do is create variations in levels on which dancers perform. For this purpose there is still the need for platforms, lifts, and flying devices.

"New Views: Life Size"   Choreography: Carol Scothorn
UCLA Dance Company   Lighting design: Doris Siegel

Marcia Roltner

Figure 6.3 Dancers moving toward an intense light source convey a sense of striving toward the point from which the light emanates.

Three-dimensionality

Much can be contributed to the three-dimensionality of a figure on the stage by approaching lighting sculpturally. Figures lit only from the front appear flat. Sidelights placed in every available entrance and at the heights of the designer's choosing, combined in differing proportions with sources from overhead, back, and front, are used to achieve a sense of depth.

Focus

Strong directional light can be used to give a sense of focus, as in Figure 6.3. Movement oriented in one direction is strengthened by dominant light coming from that direction. A dancer moving toward an intense light source conveys a sense of going or striving toward

"Mysterium"   Costume and set design: Malcolm
UCLA Dance Company   McCormick
Choreography: Marion Scott   Lighting design: Doris Siegel
                                     Dancers: Kathe Howard and Gary Bates

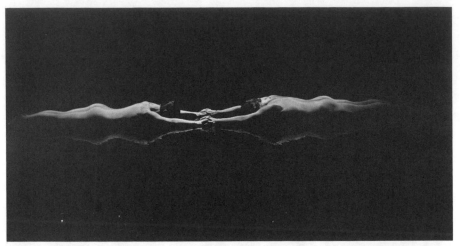

Gisela Steinmetz

Figure 6.4 Light affects the viewer's awareness of specific elements of movement and is used to highlight or emphasize those parts of the body to which special attention is to be drawn. Space defined by light does not interfere with movement and is infinitely flexible.

the point from which the light seems to emanate. On the other hand, moving away from an intense light source conveys a sense of parting, a wish to escape.

Highlighting

The direction from which light strikes a dancer draws the viewer's attention to specific elements of movement and is used to highlight or emphasize parts of the body (Figure 6.4). A movement of a dancer's back can be lost if the dancer is lighted primarily from the front. A motion of a hand conveys nothing if the hand is in darkness. A facial expression is wasted unless the face is visible to the audience.

Changes in lighting

All the elements mentioned can undergo transitions as the performance of a work progresses. The lighting designer's objective is to make the changes in lighting orchestrate the changes in choreography. With changes in lighting, the element of time is added by choice of the exact start, the duration, and the point of completion of a transition. This timing should reinforce the timing and dynamics of the movement.

Special effects created with light, such as projected images, shadows, silhouettes, and moving or flashing patterns, can be stimulating and exciting and can add theatrically to a choreographic work. When these do not grow organically out of the movement, they should be carefully considered by both choreographer and lighting designer and their dramatic effectiveness should be weighed against possible distraction from the dancer's movement.

THE LIGHTING DESIGNER FOR DANCE THEATRE

A good lighting designer for dance develops both the qualities of an artist and poet and those of a trained technician with an orderly mind and methodical approach.

The basic training must be the professional education of lighting designers for all theatrical production, which includes a thorough working knowledge of the following areas:

1. Stages, stage equipment, and terminology (see Chapter 3 and Glossary)
2. Lighting equipment, its properties and capabilities
   a. How to select or arrange instruments for the most desirable angle of light and distribution of intensity and the most suitable use of their beam spread
   b. Which instrument will give a soft-edged beam if a strong demarcation is to be avoided and "light spill" is not a problem or a sharp-edged beam if a clearly defined outline is desired
   c. Which instruments have beams that can be shaped or cut off a surface that is to be kept dark
   d. Various methods of mounting instruments
   e. Various methods of wiring and connecting instruments to circuits
   f. Types of lamps used in instruments, their burning positions and color temperatures
3. Control equipment, its properties and capabilities
   a. Availability and location of power sources in the theatre
   b. Number of outlets available, their location and capacity

    c. How the power is distributed to the outlets, directly or by way of an interconnected panel

    d. What intensity control is available to dim the light: how many controlled circuits there are, their capacity, and their ability to interconnect; knowledge of various types of boards, their operation, and their capacities for presetting, mastering, or memory storage, if any

4. Color theory and color media

    a. The effect of colored lights on colored surfaces

    b. How to mix various colors

    c. What color media are available for stage lighting: glass, plastic

    d. The available color range for these media and where to obtain them

5. Plans and plots, how to draw and read them

    a. How to present clearly on paper: instructions for the installation of equipment, specifying type and location of each instrument; instructions for connecting each instrument, showing wiring, control, and groupings; instructions for coloring, angling, and shaping of the beams

    b. How to look at plans of a theatre and interpret them correctly, or how to draw accurate plans of a theatre for the use of others

6. Theatrical working procedures, including scheduling, staffing, and the equipping of a production (see Chapter 3)

7. Co-workers, their areas of operation, duties, and concerns (how and when to correlate the process of lighting with choreographers, designers, musicians, dancers, stage manager, electricians, and crews)

8. The purpose and potentials of lighting discussed earlier

The specialization in dance lighting requires, in addition, a knowledge of various dance forms and types of dance productions. A broad acquaintance with theatre and dance history is a great asset. The position calls for a person sensitive and perceptive in specific areas. The designer must be:

- "tuned-in" to dance
- stimulated by movement through strong kinesthetic reactions
- able to enjoy and grasp abstract concepts

- attuned to dynamics, changes in dynamics, and the dynamics of change
- aware of music and other accompaniments and have an acute sensitivity to auditory stimuli and their interaction with the dance

When no one person is available with all these technical and aesthetic qualifications, two persons may be needed, persons who can communicate with each other clearly and successfully and stimulate each other in the development of a lighting concept.

Every choreographer and artistic director for dance theatre is aided immeasurably by training in the other art forms involved in the final production: music and design. The knowledge of the capabilities, language, and procedures of these areas opens the way to clear communication with a technically trained "theatre person" and makes possible the conceptual formation and achievement of aesthetic aims.

WORKING PROCEDURE OF THE LIGHTING DESIGNER

Creating the mental image

The design process can begin at various stages in the development of the work. Whether the choreographer and designer are one and the same person or two people who agree to work together from the very concept of a project, the ideas for choreography and lighting develop simultaneously. Frequently, however, the lighting designer is brought into the project when rehearsals are already in progress and at that point will start to gather all the information that will affect various choices and decisions.

Ideally, before proceeding with the design, the designer will see a complete run-through of a work with costumes, accompaniment, and scenery. Usually the rehearsal will be in a studio, possibly with completed score on tape and the costumes and scenery in sketches and swatches. The designer should see and hear a work before any consultation takes place. Verbal description or instructions by the choreographer will influence the initial reaction of the designer and severely limit the designer's ability to make a significant independent creative contribution. The lighting designer should see as many rehearsals as required to develop a clear visual concept of the work, freely discussing ideas with the choreographer after the first viewing.

A skilled choreographer will challenge the designer's creativity, incorporating the designer's suitable ideas into the work and rejecting those that are contrary to the basic choreographic concept, and will stimulate the designer to explore further ideas.

During this formative stage, communication among lighting, scenic, and costume designers is essential to coordinate all visual elements of the production, and the lighting designer must become acquainted with the facility in which the production is to take place and with the available equipment.

Putting the image on paper

With all the information gathered, the lighting designer proceeds to draw the light plot, to put the image on paper. The designer's technical knowledge is summoned to translate ideas and mental pictures into light sources, instrument mounting positions, wiring, groupings, and color media numbers.

Starting with a ground plan and section of the stage to be used, the designer proceeds to draw in light locations, making sure they are not in the audience's range of vision unless this is considered desirable. Next, the lighting instruments are drawn in to scale, located accurately on pipes and floor stands. Differing symbols are used to show the exact type and wattage of each instrument (Figure 6.5). The wiring is clearly indicated. A schedule is made giving information about each instrument, color to be used with it, the area it is to cover, the dimming circuit that will control it, and other pertinent data (Figure 6.6).

This "paper work" should be as clear and complete as possible. Whether drawn and written by hand using standard accepted symbols or generated using computer-assisted drafting and computer database programs, clear paper work makes for effective communications with co-workers and good use of theatre time.

Following the completion of the paper work, attendance by the designer at a spacing rehearsal on the actual stage to be used serves as a valuable check on the planned locations of lighting instruments to make sure that light will come from the anticipated angles. Any poorly placed instruments can be relocated on the plan. It is infinitely easier to make a change on paper than to rehang and rewire equipment on the stage.

Before moving into the theatre, the designer should think through once again each step of each work to be performed on the program to make sure that:

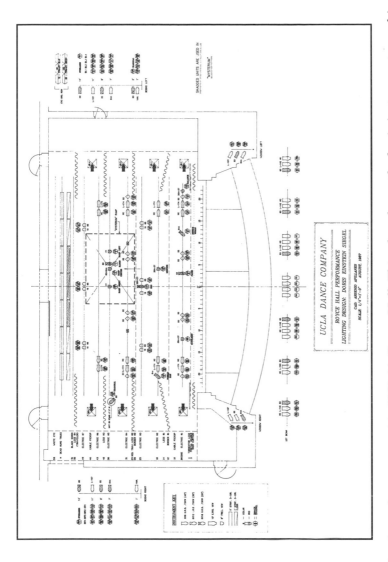

Figure 6.5 Plan for a dance concert in UCLA's Royce Hall. This plan shows the basic instruments used in the concert, and the specials for "Mysterium." Each is shown with its dimmer and channel number, as well as the color used in it. The lighting instruments used in "Mysterium" are shaded to help clarify the hook-up and cue sheets for this work (Figures 6.6 and 6.7). *Note:* Royce Hall has a dimmer-per-circuit installation. In theatres in which this is not the case, read "circuit" for "dimmer." "Channel" represents a grouping of dimmers and circuits.

Figure 6.6

Channel #	Dimmer #	Location	Type	Area	Color (Roscolux)	Function
01	171	5th Elec.	1-.75K 30° ERS (iris)	C of ramp	R-60	Opening: hands only
02	169	5th Elec.	1-1K 6" Fresnel	R side of ramp	R-77	R ramp downlight
03	172	5th Elec.	1-1K 6" Fresnel	L side of ramp	R-77	L ramp downlight
04	387	4th Ent. L 14'h	1-.75K 6×9 ERS	L streamer	R-60	Scenery light
04	394	4th Ent. R 14'h	1-.75K 6×9 ERS	R streamer	R-60	Scenery light
05	170	5th Elec.	1-1K 6" Fresnel	C of ramp	R-60 + R-64A	C ramp downlight (no feet)
06	103	1st Elec.	1-.75K 30° ERS (iris)	C of ramp	R-03	Faces only
07	88	1st Elec.	1-1K 6" Fresnel	DR	R-35A + R-37	Downlight, "together"
08	110	1st Elec.	1-.75K 30° ERS	DL	R-64A	"Mobile": woman
09	133	2nd Elec.	1-.75K 30° ERS	UR	R-64A	"Mobile": man
10	378	3rd Ent. R 2'h	1-.75K 30° ERS	UR to DL	R-60	Diagonal path
11	339	1st Ent. L 2'h	1-.75K 30° ERS	DL to UR	R-60	Diagonal path
12	129	2nd Elec.	1-1K 6" Fresnel	LC	R-35A + R-37	Downlight on faces, "meeting"
13	115	1st Elec.	1-1K 6" Fresnel	LC	R-35A + R-37	"Balance"
14	122	3rd Elec.	1-.75K 20° ERS	UC	R-35A + R-37	Turns at end

		US Floor strip	12-3K PAR floods	Cyclorama C	Primary blue	
19	191	US Floor strip	12-3K PAR floods	Cyclorama C	Primary blue	
20	192	US Floor strip	12-.3K PAR floods	Cyclorama C	Primary green	
21	40-44	Front of house	2-1K 10° ERS	DL	R-83	Blue front wash
21	50-57	Front of house	2-1K 10° ERS	DC	R-83	Blue front wash
21	61-67	Front of house	2-1K 10° ERS	DR	R-83	Blue front wash
28	268	Prosc. Window L	1-.75K 6X9 ERS	DS across	R-52	
29	277	Prosc. Window R	1-.75K 6X9 ERS	DS across	R-64A	
35	341	1st Ent. L 9'h	1-.75K 6'9 ERS	Across stage	R-52	
35	357	2nd Ent. L 9'h	1-.75K 6'9 ERS	Across stage	R-52	
36	344	1st Ent. R 9'h	1-.75K 6X9 ERS	Across stage	R-52	
36	360	2nd Ent. R 9'h	1-.75K 6X9 ERS	Across stage	R-52	
37	368	3rd Ent. L 9'h	1-.75K 6X9 ERS	Across stage	R-52	
37	389	4th Ent. L 9'h	1-.75K 6X9 ERS	Across stage	R-52	
40	345	1st Ent. R 7'h	1-.75K 6X9 ERS	Across stage	R-64A	
40	361	2nd Ent. R 7'h	1-.75K 6X9 ERS	Across stage	R-64A	
42	377	3rd Ent. R 7'h	1-.75K 6X9 ERS	Across stage	R-64A	
42	393	4th Ent. R 7'h	1-.75K 6X9 ERS	Across stage	R-64A	

Key: R = Right (stage) L = Left (stage) D or DS = Downstage U or US = Upstage C = Center (stage) ERS = Ellipsoidal Reflector Spot K = Kilowatt (1,000 watts)

Figure 6.6 Board hook-up for "Mysterium," extracted from the plot for a UCLA Dance Company concert in Royce Hall. A hook-up for a whole concert would show all the equipment used in all works. Developing the board hook-up on a computer with a database program enables the designer to sort all information (locations, type, area, coverage, colors, and functions) with ease, facilitating paper work considerably.

- Uncertainties have been resolved by observation in rehearsals, further conferences with the choreographer or other designers, or rechecking the stage or equipment
- Lighting plans—drawings, schedules, and preplanned cues—are clear, complete, and accurate
- Arrangements have been made for all required equipment
- If the equipment is limited, it is allocated to the greatest advantage
- Groupings allow for all the transitions to be made and no light sources are wired together if they might have to work separately
- Selected colors give the range of shades desired, singly or when blended together, and the color media are on hand or have been ordered

Transferring the plan from paper to stage

Transferring the plan from paper to stage is the next step in preparation for lighting rehearsals. With the start of installation in the theatre, the electrician enters the scene. The electrician and the electrical crew check that all necessary equipment is at hand and install it in the theatre exactly as indicated on the plot. They wire each instrument as indicated, prepare the colors, and make all connections on the control board as per the schedule, continuously checking all the mechanical and electrical safety of the installation. Once everything is in place, each instrument is angled and its beam shaped and color installed under the supervision of the lighting designer (Figure 6.7).

While lighting installation takes place, the stage is usually cluttered with instruments, ladders, cables, and other equipment. Obviously, it would be highly impractical to schedule any dance rehearsals here at this point unless time has been allotted for clearing and cleaning the stage.

A note on the ideal electrician: Dance lighting is often very intricate, has many changes that frequently overlap, tends to require delicate timing that may vary slightly with differences in performance, may be based on musical or auditory cues, and is rarely overrehearsed. The ideal dance theatre electrician is a good craftsperson and crew head, chooses a staff with care, is musical, has a feeling for movement, and has prior experience with dance performances. This person should be an excellent board operator who is quick, accurate,

Sam Jones

Figure 6.7 Once everything is installed and wired as indicated on the plot, each lighting instrument is angled, its beam shaped, and its color installed.

intelligent, calm, cheerful, and flexible. With the proliferation of computer boards, the running of a dance concert has become much easier once the board has been properly programmed (Figure 6.8). Fortunately, someone with all the needed abilities and qualities may feel challenged by the intricacies of dance lighting and could be enthusiastic about working the show.

Realizing the mental image

Once the installation is completed, we are ready to realize the mental image. For this to be done successfully, a number of elements are needed. The stage must be available for lighting, with no interference from extraneous light sources, such as house lights or work lights. If musicians' lights have to be on during the performance, they should also be on during the lighting session. The performance crew must be in place: board operators, spotlight operators, and anyone else concerned with lighting. The stage manager must be present and ready. The stage must be set completely for the dances

CSULB Department of Dance   Martha B. Knoebel Dance Theatre

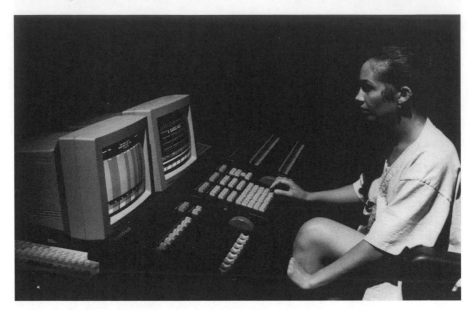

Figure 6.8 E.T.C. Obsession, a state-of-the-art computer light board in operation.

to be lighted, with all drapes, scenery, and props in place and fully painted. The dancers must be available and in costume. The lighting designer cannot weigh the visual impact of the effect of lighting on missing dancers, costumes, sets, and colors. A rehearsal tape of the sound score is of great help when timings are being established. The choreographer should be there, ready to forego a natural inclination to make movement corrections at this time, but ever watchful of the spacing of the dancers. The lighting designer is "out front," somewhere near the center of the auditorium, with a small lamp for reading plans and schedules, possibly a monitor to track a computer board, and an intercommunication connection with the stage manager and the electrician.

Now is the moment that will show whether the mental image, translated into a light plot and then installed in the theatre, will really produce the lighting on the stage that existed in the designer's mind. It is a difficult moment. It is the time when the lighting designer can design for the first time in concrete and visual, rather than mental and theoretical, terms (Figure 6.9).

Figure 6.9 Board operator views performance on stage from the control booth at the rear of the theatre.

The dance is worked through step by step, one light setting at a time. Many possibilities are explored, both in light groupings and their intensities and in timing of transitions. When a satisfactory result is achieved, the lighting "look" or cue is recorded into memory when a computer board is used. The required manual operation is recorded on paper by the electrician, the movement or music cues are noted by the stage manager, and the timing of transitions by both (Figure 6.10).

At times plans laid out on paper work well, at other times they require revisions. Slight changes in placement of equipment or color choices may be more time-effective and produce better results than an effort to make the preset installation work at all costs. Performers may have to repeat phrases many times before the best lighting solution is achieved. Light changes that appear to be generated by movement are much less noticeable to the viewer than ones that are not. The stage manager keeps the performers informed about what is happening, when and where to start, and when to stop. Although the process can be very tedious, dancers who understand its aim are remarkably patient and cooperative.

A lighting designer, having arrived at a flow of lighting that is a realization of the mental images, will want to hear and respond to

Figure 6.10

Stage preset: Black velour legs, borders, and backdrop rigged as traveler (to open 8 feet wide later)
Cyclorama upstage of backdrop (lit by ground row placed behind traveler)
Black floor covering
Ramp placed upstage, slightly left of center, covered in black (see ground plan)
Black fabric streamers from both sides of ramp leading into fourth wings on both sides of stage
Dancers on stage in opening position (see Figure 6.5)

Opening sequence: A. Houselights out
B. Music begins
C. Curtain opens (on dark stage) on second sustained flute note

Cue no.	Timing (seconds)	Stage manager's cue	Board operation	Effect
1	10	Beginning of high note	1→10	Downlight on hands only, light blue
2	10	Gong rumble starts	2-3→10 4→4	Downlight on whole ramp, blue Sidelights on streamers, light blue
3	20	2nd push in kneeling position	5→7	Downlight circle on ramp, light blue
4	10	2nd time man rises on SR side of ramp	5→10	Downlight circle to higher reading
5	5	As both begin to roll before facing downstage together	6→10	Small warm light; faces only
6	10	As both move out of "facing down-stage" position	6→0 37→4 42→4	Faces light out Upstage L sidelight up slightly in lavender Upstage R sidelight up slightly in steel blue
7A	10	As both start getting up onto their feet	37→8 42→8	Upstage R and L sidelights to higher reading

Cue no.	Timing (seconds)	Stage manager's cue	Board operation	Effect
7B	8	As both start to move down ramp	1-2-3-5 ↘ 0	All ramp downlights out
			4 ↘ 0	Streamer lights out
			21 ↗ 8	Front wash blue up
			28-29 ↗ 8	Proscenium alcove up } L: lavender R: steel blue
			35-40 ↗ 8	Downstage sides up
			37-42 ↘ 4	Upstage sides down
8	5	As they begin to turn to each other in DR position	7 ↘ 10	DR warm light up
			21 ↘ 7	Front wash blue dim slightly
			28-29 ↘ 7	
			35-40 ↘ 7	} All sidelights dim slightly
			37-42 ↘ 3½	
9	10	Quiet turning hand to hand DR (out by time they leave area)	7 ↘ 0	DR warm light out
			21 ↗ 10	Front wash blue up higher
			28-29 ↗ 10	
			35-40 ↗ 10	} All sidelights up higher
			37-42 ↗ 5	
10	5	Man slides into "mobile" position	8-9 ↗ 10	2 small isolated spots on figures downstage L and upstage R
			All others out	Rest of stage dark
11	a:5	As woman starts to slither into diagonal	10-11 ↗ 10	Diagonal path up
	b:5	Immediate follow	8-9 ↘ 0	2 isolated spots go out
12	a:5	As they pass left of center stage on diagonal	12 ↗ 10	Warm downlight on faces up
			21 ↗ 10	Front wash blue up
			35-40 ↗ 10	Downstage sidelights up
			37-42 ↗ 5	Upstage sidelights up partly
	b:5	Immediate follow	10-11 ↘ 0	Diagonal path out

Cue	Count	Action	Readings	Description
13	5	As woman starts to go up into balance on man's knees	13 ↗ 10	Warm light on "balance" up

Both start to move back toward ramp: upstage traveler opens 8 feet in center onto cyclorama

Cue	Count	Action	Readings	Description
14	10	Start of "eagle lift"	14 → 4	Warm small spot on ramp at up center stage
			2 ↗ 10	Downlight on R ramp, blue
			19 ↗ 10	Ground-row blue up full
			20 ↗ 7	Ground-row green up partly
			12-13 → 0	
			21 → 0	} Everything else out
			35-40 → 0	
			37-42 → 0	
15	5 } 10 }	As soon as cue no. 14 is complete	19-20 → 0 }	Complete fade-out, leading with cyc ground-row
			2-14 → 0 }	
Bows			2-3 ↗ 10	
			14 ↗ 4	
			19 ↗ 10	
			20 ↗ 7	
			21 ↗ 10	
			28-29 ↗ 10	
			35-40 ↗ 10	
			36 ↗ 10	
			37-42 ↗ 5	
Orchestra bow				Pit spot up
After bow				Houselight up

Figure 6.10 Light cues for "Mysterium" (UCLA Dance Company). Shown is a composite cue sheet with information developed by the lighting designer during a lighting session. It includes the data the stage manager needs to call the cues and the electrician needs to operate them. Both will develop their own way of writing their cue sheets to make them as legible and fail-proof as possible during performances.

the choreographer's reactions and get some feedback from the other designers involved. (See Diagram of Production Personnel, Preface p. 2, showing how these functions are related.)

With luck, the dances can be run through completely, with accompaniment, before the lighting session ends, to give everyone a sense of the overall effect of the lighting and to give the stage manager and electricians a feel for the actual timing of their operations.

The facilities needed and the number of people involved in realizing the lighting designer's conceptions often result in pressure to minimize this aspect of the production time. It goes without saying that a lighting designer is expected to be well prepared for this session and to conduct it with efficiency and concentration. Yet the lighting designer must often fight for the time needed to do a good job. A knowledgeable choreographer will strongly support the lighting designer in this time requirement, knowing success depends on it.

Refining the flow of lighting

Technical and dress rehearsals are used for refining the flow of the lighting. The stage manager rechecks the sequence of cues and finds the appropriate warnings and exact signals for them. Electricians rehearse the operations they must perform during a show. The lighting designer may refine timing and intensity readings, smooth out rough spots, and make minor corrections or necessary adjustments in case of changes made in the production. A tracking sheet provides an easy-to-read overview of the flow of the lighting in a dance (Figure 6.11). It is especially useful when changes need to be made after the initial lighting session. These adjustments are made keeping in mind the capabilities and experience of your staff and the dangers inherent in major last-minute changes that cannot be rehearsed adequately by stage manager and crew and can cause serious, damaging mistakes during a performance. Even a brilliant production team works best with a last full rehearsal for a difficult show.

A note on the ideal stage manager: Knowledge of the role and craft of the stage manager (meaning a thorough acquaintance with the craft of everyone else involved with the production) and a sensitivity to movement are invaluable assets to the stage manager for dance theatre. The stage manager keeps all designers informed of all changes that might affect their plans and helps to schedule the production realistically, giving everyone the opportunity to work effectively. From the lighting designer's point of view, the stage manager

Figure 6.11

Memory #			101	102	103
Cue #			1	2	3
Timing in seconds			10	10	20
Channel #	**Function**		%	%	%
01	Opening: hands only	R-60	100	100	100
02	Ramp R downlight	R-77		100	100
03	Ramp L downlight	R-77		100	100
04	Scenic swags light	R-60		40	40
05	Ramp C downlight	R60 + 64A			70
06	Faces (on ramp)	R-03			
07	DR "together" light	RA35A + 37			
08	"Mobile": woman	R-64A			
09	"Mobile": man	R-64A			
10	Diagonal path	R-60			
11	Diagonal path	R-60			
12	"Meeting" faces	R35A + 37			
13	"Balance"	R35A + 37			
14	Turns at end	R35A + 37			
19	Cyclorama center	blue			
20	Cyclorama center	green			
21	Frontlight wash	R-83			
28	Prosc. window L	R-52			
29	Prosc. window R	R64A			
35	L 1-2 9'h:	R-52			
36	R 1-2 9'h:	R-52			
37	L 3-4 9'h:	R-52			
40	R 1-2 7'h:	R-64A			
42	R 3-4 7'h:	R-64A			

104	105	106	107	107.5	108	109	110	111.1	111.2	112.1	112.2	113	114	115	116
4	5	6	7A	7B	8	9	10	11		12		13	14	15	BOWS
10	5	10	10	8	5	10	5	5	5	5	5	5	10	5/10	
%	%	%	%	%	%	%	%	%	%	%	%	%	%	%	%
100	100	100	100												
100	100	100	100										100		100
100	100	100	100												100
40	40	40	40												
100	100	100	100												
	100														
				100											
							100	100							
							100	100							
								100	100	100					
								100	100	100					
										100	100	100			
											100				
													40		40
													100		100
													70		70
				80	70	100				100	100	100			100
				80	70	100									100
				80	70	100									100
				80	70	100				100	100	100			100
															100
		40	80	40	35	50				50	50	50			50
				80	70	100				100	100	100			100
		40	80	40	35	50				50	50	50			50

Figure 6.11 Tracking sheet for "Mysterium" (UCLA Dance Company). Intensities can be expressed in percentages, as shown here, or in whatever calibration is found on the control board being used.

should be someone who can grasp a verbal description of what the lighting designer hopes to do, take notes on possible transitions and changes (cues), and help work out their timing. During the lighting session, the stage manager catches changes in the original plans, easing the process of experimentation by keeping everyone on and off the stage alert, cheerful, and informed, making sure all operations are properly recorded before work proceeds. At subsequent rehearsals, the stage manager catches changes and refinements, ensures that the information is disseminated to all concerned, gives cues with great accuracy, knows the dances well enough to see variations in timing, spacing, or action, and can anticipate potential technical problems that may result. The stage manager knows and understands the lighting setup and the lighting for any point in the dance; he or she will spot discrepancies during performances and try to correct them or compensate for them if they occur because of equipment failure. Ultimately, the successful execution of your design during performances lies in the hands of the stage manager.

The performance

The performance may be the most trying time for a lighting designer. The role completed, the designer watches as the works are performed and hopes that everything goes as smoothly as conceived and rehearsed. Observing the total impact of the performance on the audience, one can only try to analyze one's contribution to it.

Does the lighting:

- Catch the mood and spirits of the piece and enhance it?
- Help in distilling and clarifying the structure of the piece for the audience?
- Show that the designer has sensed the dynamics of the piece?
- Reinforce the choreographer's basic intentions by placing emphasis on specific elements of the work?
- Catch all the movement highlights and expressions and help draw the viewers eyes and attention to them, making them sculpturally and visually as intense as possible?
- Create a sense of space? Of time?
- Show the sets to advantage? The costumes?

Do the light changes flow with the movement, or are they noticeable as a separate entity? In short, does the lighting support, enhance, clarify, and reinforce the concept of the choreographer as

"Mirror Mirror"   Setting and costumes: Charles Berliner
UCLA Dance Company   Lighting design: Doris Siegel
Choreography: Carol Scothorn   Dancers: Susie Goldman and Noel Reiss

Gisela Steinmetz

Figure 6.12 The double-image effect was created by dancing on a Mylar surface (a reflective plastic material.) To achieve the desired effect, the lighting had to be confined to the performers. Light hitting the reflective surface would have weakened the image.

well as that of the composer and all other designers working on the piece of choreography, or has it gone off on a frolic of its own?

Dance theatre is a coordinated effort of many artists who, unlike novelists or painters, cannot work by themselves or please themselves alone. They work together and interact to convey a unified concept, as in Figure 6.12. The process can be difficult, but the satisfaction of a work well done and the sense of communal accomplishment and exhilaration at its success can be thrilling and unforgettable.

SOURCES

Manufacturers of equipment

- Strand Lighting, 18111 South Santa Fe Avenue, P.O.Box 9004, Rancho Dominguez, CA 90221
- Altman Stage Lighting Company, 57 Alexander Street, Yonkers, NY 10701
- Colortran, Inc., P.O. Box 635, Wilsonville, OR 97070
- Electronic Theatre Controls, Inc., 3030 Laura Lane, Middleton, WI 53562

Trade magazines and publications

- *Theatre Design and Technology*, 6443 Ridings Road, Syracuse, NY 13206-1111
- *TCI* (formerly *Theatre Crafts*), 32 West 18th Street, New York, NY 10011-4612
- *Lighting Dimensions*, 32 West 18th Street, New York, NY 10011-4612

Color Media (usually available from local distributors)

- Great American Market (GAM), 826 North Cole Avenue, Hollywood, CA 90038
- Lee Filters, 1015 Chestnut Street, Burbank, CA 91506-9983
- Rosco, 36 Bush Avenue, Port Chester, NY 10573

7 . Programming and Programs

VIRGINIA FREEMAN   *Freelance choreographer. Director for dance theatre and opera including Arena Stage, Wolf Trap Opera, and the University of Maryland's graduate Opera Studio.*

This chapter reviews the factors to be considered in programming a dance concert and gives suggestions for creating balanced and interesting programs. Programming (or sequencing) a dance concert comes down to using your own good taste. There is no true equation, and there are too many exceptions to make fast rules.

Beginning programmers should start by remembering all the dance concerts they have experienced as either audience or performer. What made an evening pleasurable? What was irritating? What should you avoid? Often it is easier for a beginner to identify the negatives—the things you hope *your* audience will never have to experience—than the positive aspects of a program. Let us begin by examining some of the pitfalls of hasty or poor programming.

PROGRAMMING PITFALLS

Two common mistakes made by programmers are (1) too many short pieces, leading to too many breaks in the evening, and (2) not enough contrast between the types of performances.

If the curtain goes up and down ten or twelve times, you lose the audience. If, however, you break up the hypnotic effect of the "house lights out–curtain up curtain down–applause–house lights up" and blend some of those shorter compositions into a longer unit, you will have improved the program. For example, if you have two or three pieces that use props as obstacles, use *Obstacles* as the overall title and unrelated subtitles for dances that might include a solo with a chair, a quartet with boxes on the feet, and a duet with neck skirts flowing to the floor (no arms). The actual number of pieces may still be the same, but the audience will feel that there are fewer events.

105

If, by changing the order of the dances, you are able to shorten the time between them so that the waiting time is reduced to a minimum, it will benefit the audience and the choreographer. An audience that has not had to chitchat its way through costume/makeup changes or through an elaborate set of changes that might have been done at intermission will be a more receptive audience that is more likely to return next season.

If the pieces in the concert are all dramatic, all the same length, or all jazzy, the outcome is obvious. A bland or frenetic sameness creates the blahs; the program seems barren. Contrast, the byword in programming, will make it easier for the audience to enjoy the evening; consequently, they will be better able to judge and enjoy each individual dance. Unfortunately, everyone has survived dance concerts with only women performers, only leotard and tights for costumes, or only solo dancers whose performances all seem to end downstage left with a blackout. Given the economic realities that all dance performers face, there are still ample opportunities to vary the program both visually and conceptually in a dance evening.

CONSIDERATIONS FOR EFFECTIVE PROGRAMMING

Once the negatives have been eliminated, you should be able to make sensible programming decisions. Otherwise you might just as well say, "You go first, okay?"

Usually, no one wants to be first on a program. There is a persistent idea that the first piece is a "throwaway." *Overcome that thought!* A choreographer also may not want to begin a program with a significant piece because of the nagging notion that American audiences are notorious about arriving late. The contradiction is that an audience (especially one still new to dance) needs to be caught up by the opening piece. On the other hand, deciding how to end the program also has risks. Critics sometimes leave early to make deadlines or have had enough after a slow-paced hour and a half.

Think about the beginning and ending of the evening as you would the beginning and ending of a composition. I have opened a student concert with a choreographed movement event in five windows of the auditorium as the audience was being seated. As this event developed, the window curtains closed one at a time while the dancers came down to finish the piece on the edge of the stage as the house lights went out. This brought focus to the stage area, and the program was underway.

Try to open your program with a short piece so that no latecomers are seated during it. You will be helping to educate audiences as well as providing a pleasurable experience for those who came on time. Of course, exceptions come to mind. First, longer and longer works are being accepted in the theatre, and you may not have a good, short opening piece. Work out at what intervals in a long opening piece latecomers could be allowed into the auditorium. Second, suppose the opening piece does not happen on stage. It could start out in the lobby, in the auditorium, or even on stage before the audience is fully aware that the concert has begun. Latecomers would then be inconspicuous.

Whether you should have one or two or no intermissions should depend on physical logistics (shifting scenery, changing costumes and makeup, and arranging musicians). Choreographed movement events could be taking place during intermission other than on stage. Do not be locked into how programs "used to be" put together. An Intermission listed on a program usually means a trip to the lobby for refreshments and conversation, whereas the word Pause may keep the audience seated. More and more often the length of the intermission or the pause will also be listed on the program.

A couple of rules of thumb should be mentioned. You should plan for a shorter second half of the program. This is standard in the theatre and audiences expect it. Another is that about forty-five minutes of actual choreography easily make a one-and-a-half hour program, a desirable length. Some audiences may be willing to sit longer, but not if the additional time is owing to a late start or lengthy breaks.

Doris Humphrey warned choreographers not to compose the end of the dance last. This also holds true in programming. Do not wait until the last minute to discover that you really do not have a good piece with which to end your concert. Think ahead. Also do not get stuck with the "you can't end with a solo" thought. Why not? A solo may be just the thing. Audiences do not demand an old-time finale, but in programming do remember that the last piece should be striking, be it group or solo. Audiences remember the last piece as they walk out. It may be the first thing an audience that is new to dance talks about, and all of us should recognize that we are doing a public-relations job in building future dance audiences.

Try a rough run-through of a possible program order in the studio even before your choreographers have finished pieces and especially before programs go to the printer or photocopy machine. You may discover problems, and it will help the whole group to see and hear what goes on in your artistic director's decision-making head. There may still be time to try another sequence or revive something from last year's repertory that fills a void or really works as an opening if this year's crop does not produce one. This may be the time to think about adding a local guest artist for contrast or to help cover those "costume-waits" of your own group.

PROGRAMS

The fashion of yesterday of making "essence titles," one-, two-, or three-word poetic gems, may make a unified program page with title on one side and music on the other. For example:

Reunion . . . . Jones

However, you can use the space differently if, instead of calling a piece "Reunion," you decide on (as in folk song) the following:

Take One Step in My Direction
and I'll Take Two in Yours . . . . . Jones

See Figure 7.1 for an example of two formats for the same dance, one using a subtitle. "Dead Reckoning" (a navigational term) was the title for a dance about Amelia Earhart and the search to find her.

Once pieces are titled and the order is set, it is time to plan how the program will look on paper. Format, size, color, print, cover, and design should be determined in consultation with a graphic artist, budget permitting. If not, much can be done with stylus, stencil, press-on letters, computer, and photocopy machine to see how the final copy will look.

Make a folded, lap-sized program because full sheets stapled together are sure to slide off and be difficult to handle. Try folding the usual 8 1/2" × 11" sheets the long, narrow way if the titles are short ones. Take time to print it out several ways and let your eye be the judge. Select an attractive paper color that goes well with the type. Note that papers in reds and darker blues make difficult reading with black type, so stay with the lighter or more electric shades. If the budget allows, pick a darker shade of print against a lighter shade of paper of the same color—but check how it looks before you have all the programs printed. I remember once picking nice purple ink on a pale lavender paper, only to discover that the combination looked much like the usual purple ditto sheets (minus the smears)

DEAD RECKONING

"Head winds .... half an hour's gas .... circling ...."

Earhart's final message

Choreography: Virginia Freeman

Music: Charles Ives' *The Unanswered Question*

Script: Susan Galbraith

Repertory Class Performers: Renee Ioppini, Anne Rohrs, Nancy Sullivan. Alternates — Kathy Carter-Winting, Janis Yamor

Dead Reckoning (1977)

Choreography	Virginia Freeman
Music	Charles Ives' The Unanswered Question
Script	Susan Galbraith
Voice	Anne Stone
Costumes	Dorritt Carroll
Lighting	Michael J. Foley

Danced by

Andrea Price   Libby Wade   Della Weinheimer

Figure 7.1 Two program formats.

SONATAS *(Premiere)*
Choreography: Jeff Slayton
Music: Alessandro Scarlatti
Costumes: Michael Pacciorini
Dancers: Julia Bullock, Roxanne Narachi*, Margaret Molinatti, Shelley Culp, Michelle DePriest, Laurie Morin

A MEANDER (FOR TWO) *(Premiere)*
Choreography: Tryntje Shapli
Music: Lisbeth Woodies
Text: Irish Traditional (11th Century)
     Read by Omar Shapli
Costumes: Nancy Jo Smith
Dancers: Gina Balladone, June Gais Moscov
The dance is based on images found in THE BOOK OF KELLS, a 7th or 8th Century Irish Manuscript.

OUT IN EXISTENCE *(Premiere)*
Choreography: Sandra Shahrivar**
Music: Ruby Abeling
Costumes: Cynthia Thompson
Dancers: Michelle DePriest, Stacey Lyons

NINE PERSON PRECISION BALL PASSING (1975)
Choreography: Charles Moulton
Music: A Leroy
Costumes: Michael Pacciorini
Dancers: Kiersten Brooks, Julia Bullock, CatherineMarie Davalos, Greg Kirkman, Kerri Kimball, Leanne Lacazotte, Steve Levy, June Gais Moscov, Oscar-Kim Salomons

INTERMISSION

VALENTINE (1971)
Choreography: Gerald Arpino
Re-staged and directed by Rebecca Wright
Music: Jacob Druckman
Contrabass: Bertram Turetzky
Dancers' costumes and set: Courtesy of The Joffrey Ballet
Robes and Mr. Turetzky's costume: Nancy Jo Smith
Dancers: Gina Balladone, Andy Kwan

ISSUE (1975)
Choreography: Rachel Lampert
Re-staged and directed by Holly Harbinger
Music: Ivanovici
Costumes: Nancy Jo Smith
Dancers: The Mother   Roxanne Narachi*
         The Father   Sean Sullivan
         The Child   CatherineMarie Davalos

AND SHE WAS (1987)
Choreography: Nora Reynolds
Music: Collage
Costumes: Nancy Jo Smith
Dancers: Mila Abitria, Deirdre Owen, Shelley Culp, Ona Cheravalos, Marina Panossian

* Recipient of the 1986 Fine Arts Affiliates Scholarship in Dance.
** Recipient of the 1986-87 Dramatic Allied Arts Guild Scholarship in Dance.
† Recipient of the 1987 Lillian Newman Komaroff Award in Dance.

Figure 7.2 Sample dance concert program.

available then in most school offices. The computer age is here to help you to cut costs and be more flexible.

Coming back to the layout, trust your own eye to balance the pages. By using different sizes of print, by typing all capital letters, or by underlining you can set the title off from any program note or subtitled sections under it. The title is usually in the left margin, with the music credits on the same line in the right margin. The choreographer and dancers are spaced below the title. I tend to lean toward listing the choreographer first, followed by the dancers' names. Be as consistent as possible throughout in listing all the credits.

Music credits usually include composers' names and no identification of the selection. Many feel that the last name is enough, especially with well-known artists such as Bach, Bartok, or Brubeck. Others prefer whole names. (Figure 7.1 shows use of the composer's complete name as well as the title of the music.) When a commissioned score is used, the composer's name should appear in full. There also should be a program footnote or a note on the credit page. Special note should be made of scores that have been "assembled," either by listing all the composers involved, by "tape collage," or just "collage" (see Figure 7.2, "And She Was").

Consistency should govern the listing of costume design and sets. They should appear under the dance or on the credit page.

As shown in Figure 7.2, type size and style may be varied for emphasis or clarity. If a dance is a premiere performance, say so. If it is an older dance, you might list in parentheses the year it was choreographed (see "Valentine" in Figure 7.2).

Following are some program "extras," items often included on a dance program:

- Biographies of contributing artists (choreographers, dancers, musicians, designers); keep all to approximately the same length, and use a parallel format
- Coming dance events (see Figure 7.3)
- Introduction to sponsoring group (Figure 7.3): describe functions, invite participation and/or contributions, offer placement on a mailing list
- Credits and acknowledgments: list production staff (Figure 7.3); recognize donors in the program or on an insert page. (Do not overdo; a thank-you note may be more appropriate than having a lengthy list of names that clutter a program)

PRODUCTION STAFF

Production Coordinator . . . . Jeff Slayton
Music Director . . . . Ruby Abeling
Lighting Design / Technical Director . . . . R. Craig Wolf
Costume Design . . . . Nancy Jo Smith
Cynthia Thompson, Michael Pacciorini
Stage Manager . . . . Debra Styer
Costume Construction Assistant . . . . Cynthia Thompson
Assistant Lighting Designer . . . . Allyson McCullough

Production Crew: Caroline Russell, Elizabeth Medina, Jeannie Manapol, Tracy Cummins, Andre DeLeon, Susan DuBois, Angel Quesada

Costume Crew: Sandra Nadeau, Kymberlee Hill, Patricia Gaines, Lamont Sims-Bey, Laurie Morin, Juan Betancourt

Production Assistant . . . . Cheryl Case
House Manager . . . . Felicia Jackson
Program Design . . . . Dan Sweetman
Visual Communication Design Workshop

FACULTY – DEPARTMENT OF DANCE

Joan Schlaich–Chair, Pat Finot, Celeste Kennedy, Tryntje Shapli, Jeff Slayton, Vicki Angel, Mary Jane Eisenberg, Pamela Fairweather, Pauline Hagino, Bruce Heath, Betty Martyn, Gloria Newman, Kathleen Owens, Michele Simmons, Florence Stiles, Gennie Strauss, David Wilcox. MUSICIANS: Ruby Abeling, Eric Ruskin, Lisbeth Woodies. STAFF: Kim Rourke.

THE DEPARTMENT OF DANCE offers a B.A. program with emphasis in modern dance. Courses include modern, ballet, jazz and tap techniques, composition, notation, kinesiology, history of dance, dance production, lighting for dance and music for dance. The program centers around a core of required courses, and includes a range of electives. For more information, write to the Dance Department, California State University, Long Beach, CA. 90840.

COMING EVENTS

Scholarship Auditions for the CSU Summer Arts . . . . May 2
TA-241, 1–3 PM
Intermedia Festival (CSULB Dance and Music Departments) . . . . May 13, 14
University Theatre, 8 PM

If you would like to be on the Dance Mailing List please fill out a pink card in the foyer.

Figure 7.3 Extract from concert program with staff listing and department announcements.

- Commissioned dances: credit with a program note or asterisked footnote
- Student scholarships and awards: you could asterisk names, as in Figure 7.2
- Program notes (see "A Meander (For Two)" in Figure 7.2)

Spelling of names of choreographers, dancers, and production crew should be carefully reviewed; have all participants check their own names.

Once the program content is set, there are three ways to produce the actual program: (1) photocopying; (2) professional printing; (3) using a computer with a letter-quality printer (usually for a small number). The first two methods require a cleanly and accurately produced copy of the program. The choice of reproduction method depends on budget and need.

An attractive program posted on a bulletin board at schools and theatres is good promotion for this and future performances.

8 . Makeup

BARBARA MATTHEWS *Instructor and director of makeup design, Department of Theatre Arts, California State University, Long Beach.*

Makeup has been an integral part of dance since primitive times. Indeed, we have come to expect a certain stylized look with this art form, and we are often disappointed when this visual expectation is not met. As aesthetics change, however, so must techniques and attitudes. We can maintain the integrity of the total dance art form and still create a provocative and visually stunning look by following the basic principles of makeup. It is the intent of this chapter to guide dancers through the steps needed to achieve the "dance look" as well as to enhance their own features on the stage.

There are several factors to consider when applying makeup for dance production. First and foremost is to discover if there is a makeup designer who has done the work for you. If not, which is more likely, you are on your own and must take into account such matters as the color and style of your costume, how many dance pieces you are in, if there are fast makeup/hair changes between pieces, the color gels that are used for lighting, if this is an ensemble piece, any special makeup/hair requirements, the best makeup to use, how long it takes to apply makeup, if body makeup is needed, and so forth. We will examine the specific needs of dance makeup and in doing so address many of these concerns.

PREPARATION AND MATERIALS

A clean face is essential before you apply makeup. There are no magic skin-care products for the performer, so whatever is your personal preference and produces the best results for you should be fine. If you moisturize, however, it is best to do so at least a half-hour before applying your makeup, as theatrical makeup does not adhere well to overly moist or oily skin. A good toning lotion or astringent, such as witch hazel or Sea Breeze, is helpful before you apply foundation. In order to maintain healthy skin it is equally important to remove your makeup properly after every performance. There are several good makeup removers available, and the one best suited for you may depend on which type of makeup you use. Do remember, however, that soap and water are not adequate, as they merely remove the top layer and never deep-cleanse the skin. Cold creams and cleansing lotions are better. For an occasional quick removal before thorough cleansing, or for a fast makeup change during performance between dance pieces, disposable "baby wipes" can come in very handy. Just as in your daily routine, sensible skin care during production will serve you best.

FOUNDATION

As the name indicates, this is applied first. Also known as "base" or "base color," foundation serves to enhance the dancer's appearance under stage lighting as well as even out the skin tones. It also helps the rest of the makeup, such as contour and blush, to go on smoother. There are different types of foundation but some are not as suitable for dance as others.

Creme foundations are ideal for dance as they are generally quite saturated with color and provide stronger coverage. Unlike liquid or water-soluble pancake makeup, creme foundations tend to hold up better to the heat of the lighting instruments and the rigorous demands of physical movement. Remember that all creme makeup *must* be set with a translucent powder, which absorbs oils and moisture and retards perspiration to create a matte finish. Lose that shine!

In selecting your base color, consider the size of the stage, your skin color, and lights. As a rule of thumb, but in no way gospel, a foundation slightly darker than your natural color would be used for Caucasians, whereas a foundation that matches your natural color is best suited for African-American, Asian, and Hispanic skin tones. For fantasy, surreal, or stylized makeup, color choice will depend on the specific needs of the artistic concept. If the situation permits, it is helpful to sample your base color under the lights that will be used during performance. This may have to wait until dress rehearsal, but even so, take advantage of the opportunity. Makeup is affected dramatically by lighting, and the finished product will look quite different on the stage than it does in the dressing room.

To apply creme base, use a foam-rubber (latex) sponge and wash it after each use. You will get a few uses before the sponge starts to crumble; when you are getting more rubber crumbs on your face than foundation, it is time for a new sponge. They are quite inexpensive and are often sold in bulk. Use the sponge to pick up a bit of the makeup and apply it to different areas of the face. With a gentle touch "tap" and "pull" the makeup to blend evenly over the entire face. Remember to fade down and blend the color onto the neck (and the ears if they show). The expressions "tap" and "pull" are used so that you are aware that you need not apply base with a heavy hand or as if you were using a trowel. The purpose is to even out the skin tone, cover any imperfections, and add enough color so that you do not appear washed out under stage lights. You are striving for a smooth, not a caked, look. In makeup application, remember that less is more, and you can always add if there is not enough color.

Depending on which company's makeup you use, there are various shades (and names) for the same color. There are theatrical makeup manufacturers, readily available in most areas of the country, that offer basic kits at good value (see Sources). These kits generally give you everything you need to complete a makeup design. You will often find these brands for sale at local theatrical supply houses or you can order them directly from the company. Remember, these are only a few of the very fine theatrical makeup lines. Naturally, you can supplement them with some favorite items of your own, for example, a good blush brush or some powder eye shadows. Many of these added items can be purchased at your local drug or department stores. Makeup can be mix-and-match provided it looks good in the end and achieves the desired effect. Colors can also be mixed to provide you with the exact shade you need if you do not already have it. Sometimes it is necessary to experiment with makeup before actually applying it, especially if you are using a new brand or different tools for the first time.

Body makeup may be called for from time to time, either as a necessary design element or simply to match the color that has been used as foundation on the face. Generally speaking, body makeup is a pancake (dry powder) or a liquid made from powder rather than creme and is usually applied with a medium to fairly large natural sponge (not a latex sponge). Unless you are directed differently, match the body makeup color to that of your foundation. More often than not, manufacturers have corresponding names or numbers of foundations and body makeup. When applying body makeup, you generally use large strokes with a slightly dampened sponge, blending any edges as you go so that you do not have huge streaks on your chest, legs, or arms. If the final result looks a bit chalky, you can buff the area with a soft cloth (silk) or a very lightly moistened chamois. Remember to make up your hands (and the tops of your feet if dancing barefoot) so they do not read as pale from the stage. If full body makeup is not needed, but a warm glow or hint of color would add to the overall look, a light dusting of bronzing powder over the paler areas of the body may be a nice touch. Most cosmetic lines offer light, medium, or dark shades of bronzing powder.

CONTOUR

The purpose of contouring is to improve or change the facial structure as well as to give it dimension from the distance of the stage. This is accomplished through the basic principles of shading and highlighting. Shading makes a feature less noticeable. Highlighting accentuates it. Generally, shadow with a color two to three shades darker than your foundation and highlight with pale shades two to three shades lighter than your foundation. You can even use extremes of color, provided that you blend and fade. Through the proper use of highlight and shadow, you will be amazed at the illu-

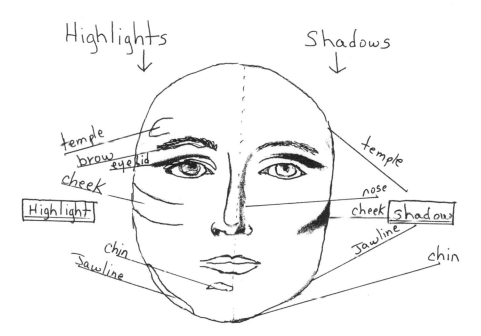

Figure 8.1 Contour shading.

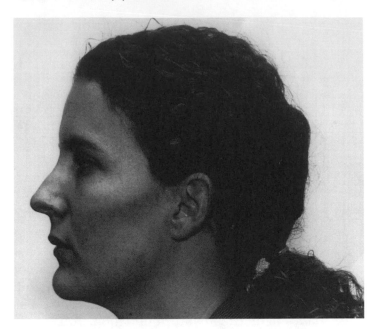

Figure 8.2 Contours.

sion you can create. However, remember that you are creating an illusion, not performing cosmetic surgery. There is only so much you can do with makeup to alter the appearance of your facial structure. From the stage, you can create the illusion of different dimensions to your face, thereby giving the sense of an altered and, hopefully, improved appearance.

Techniques (and opinions) differ on the best way to apply contour. Look for the easiest and quickest method as long as it produces the desired effect. Eventually, you will find what is most efficient for you. Because they are easy to see instantly, begin by contouring the larger areas of the face (cheeks and jawline). Then work to the smaller ones, such as the nose and eyes (Figures 8.1 and 8.2).

Cheeks and jawline

The placement of the cheekbone contour is crucial. It is often this poorly positioned and heavily applied shadow that gives dancers a dirty or bruised look. To help locate the correct placement of this contour, suck in your cheeks and press your fingertips gently under the cheekbone until you feel the hollow area. With your fingertips underneath the bone, follow the sunken area back until it meets with the little curved protrusion in front of the ear. This motion of the fingers will now be repeated in the reverse direction with the makeup.

Beginning in front of the ear protrusion, with a wedged sponge or the fingertips (or a brush if you use powder) apply a small amount of shadow and follow the slight curve along the hollow until you are aligned with the outer corner of your eye. Always leave a tapering off at the end of your shadow line rather than a blunt mark. Then, with a downward motion (toward the jaw) feather and fade the shadow to approximately one-and-one-half fingers' width, leaving the intensity of the shadow darkest just under the cheekbone and gradually becoming lighter as you move downward, but never reaching the jawbone. If the initial line of shadow still looks harsh, you may want to diffuse (gently tap) the top part of the contour line so that the makeup does not read like a streak on the cheek. The purpose of all this blending is to keep the shadow from looking like you are painting the broad side of a barn. (See Figures 8.1 and 8.2.) This principle holds true whether you are making up for everyday use, a small theatre, or Lincoln Center; only the intensity of the makeup differs.

You should also add shadow along the jawline to give it definition and dimension. Start shadowing below the ear and extend the shadow under the jawbone. Fade this down so that it does not read like a line. You may also want to add a little shadow at the point of the chin or, if you have a cleft, accent it with shadow.

After shadowing certain areas of the face, it is now essential to add highlights to create dimension and avoid having the face appear flat. Add highlight on the cheekbones and smooth it back on the bone toward the hairline. You should now notice the prominence of your high cheekbones, often a desirable aesthetic from the stage. Then, lightly highlight the jawline (above the shadow you added on the jawbone), fading it as it moves forward. (See Figures 8.1 and 8.2.)

As for individual needs, it is best to remember the basic guidelines of contouring: shadow makes things appear smaller, more recessed, or less noticeable; highlight gives the illusion of being more prominent, larger, or more noticeable. For example, if you have a square jawline and want to create a more oval shape, apply shadow along the jawbone and blend upward to the area you want to minimize. Or, if you have a broad forehead and want to narrow it, place shadow at the temples and then fade toward the hairline and soften the color. Oftentimes you can find the correct placement of your shadow by laying your fingers as an imaginary template over the area that you want to deaccentuate and then placing shadow there. Be careful that you do not leave unblended lines because you will draw more attention to the exact area that you want to be less noticeable. Use Figures 8.1 and 8.2 as a guideline for the areas to be contoured, making adjustments to your own face as needed.

Nose

Any changes to the nose will be effective only from a front view, since an altered profile would require an added three-dimensional piece. However, you can achieve the illusion of a shorter, narrower, longer, wider, or even a straighter nose by placing highlights in the areas that you want to attract attention to and shadowing the areas that you want to make less noticeable or want to appear smaller than they actually are. For example, if you want the nose to appear shorter, apply a shadow under the tip and blend upward over the tip, then add a small highlight on the upper part of the nose to create the illusion of a shorter bridge. Obviously, the converse of this technique would be used to create a longer nose. If you want to narrow the nose, shadow the sides of the nose in a straight line (remember to blend the edges) and add a narrow highlight down the center. If you do not wish to alter your nose, simply apply lines of shadow down the sides of the bridge and add a little highlight down the center. Remember to fade.

Eyes

As the most expressive part of the face, the eyes need to be enhanced for a stage appearance. It is not always ideal to follow the fashion trends of the day concerning the application of eye makeup, as this may not flatter the wearer. The intent of eye makeup is to draw attention to the eye and make it appear larger. Naturally, there are many different eye shapes, so that adjustments must be made to accommodate each. But as a guideline for dance makeup, there are certain principles that correctly applied offer the wonderfully theatrical look of "the dancer."

Use a pale or even white eye shadow across the entire eyelid. If you are using powder eye shadow, a slightly frosted type offers a brighter highlight that helps to create the illusion of a larger eye. If this

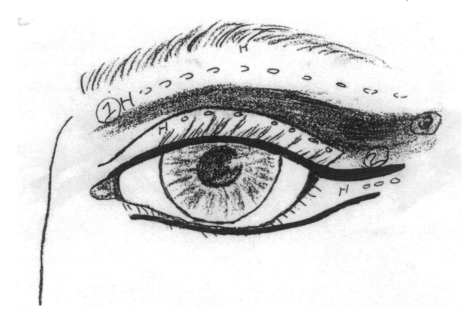

Figure 8.3 Eyeliner: 1. H = highlight ⊃⊃⊃; 2. Line lashes; 3. Shadow crease.

looks too glittery or shimmery on the whole eyelid, use the frosted eye shadow in the center of the eyelid over a matte highlight. Remember, you can also use creme eye shadows, but make sure you powder well.

Next, using a cake or liquid eyeliner draw a thin line on the top eyelid right along the lash line with a slight extension at the outer corner, as if an imaginary line were being drawn toward the eyebrow. Fade the line at the inner corner of the eye. Be careful that this line does not get too thick or it will close in the eye and defeat the purpose of the highlight. Then, under the eye, draw a straight line slightly past the outer corner but do not take it as far as the top line and do not close them together. (See Figures 8.3 and 8.4.) The intention is to create a new width and height to the eye. You generally add the same highlight color used on your eyelid to the space between the two lines in the outer corner of your eye.

Next, apply a dark eye shadow to the shadow crease (the space above the eyelid but below the eye socket bone). Rather than following the shape of your bone, which naturally slopes downward, allow the eye shadow to extend beyond the eye so that it also follows the shape of the eyeliner that you added to your eyelid. (See

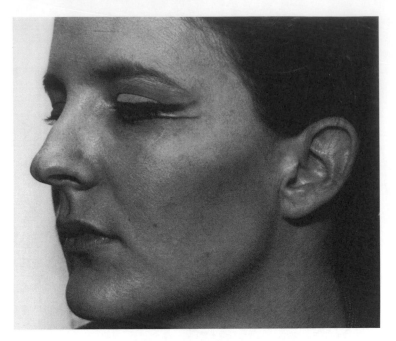

Figure 8.4 Eyeliner.

Figures 8.3 and 8.4.) If you want a more dramatic look or to add some other color to the eye, use a dark eye shadow to create the contour in the shadow crease, and then blend in a lighter eye shadow and lightly fade toward the eyebrow. To give a lift to the entire eye area, add a bright highlight just under the arch of the eyebrow.

Finally, to complete the eye makeup, add false eyelashes (only if you are comfortable with them), or at the very least add thick mascara. Give definition to your eyebrows by filling out or reshaping them. Use a pencil with short, light strokes or a pressed eye shadow with an angled brush. The key here, of course, is to keep a natural look unless the desired goal is something more extreme. However, if you have very light hair and eyebrows, you will want to darken the brow with a color that will look natural on your face. Changing the shape or giving an arch can be very effective in opening the eye and can be very attractive and natural if done properly. You can practice drawing light strokes on your hand before you actually work on your brow. Eyebrows should be as long as the eyeliner so that the entire eye area looks like a unit. Generally for women the brow tapers slightly at the end. (See Figures 8.3 and 8.4.)

Here are some tips for the most common errors when applying eye makeup:

- Tap off any excess eye shadow from the brush before applying it to the eye. This is also a good practice for contour or blush when using powder makeup; better too much on the floor than on your face.
- When using a powder eye shadow, hold a tissue under your eye to catch any of the powder flakes, especially when using dark shadows.
- If you use eyeliner pencils and they keep breaking when being sharpened, try putting them in the freezer for a few minutes.
- If you curl your eyelashes, curl them before you apply mascara.
- As in any instance with makeup application, if you mess up, a Q-tip dipped in gentle eye-makeup remover can take care of most mistakes.

Lips

For the face to look unified, the intensity of the eye must be balanced with the proper color and shape of the lips. Lip color should be complementary to your blush and costume, and, needless to say, your own skin color. You can change the shape of your lips with liner. However, if you reshape the upper lip to make it appear fuller, you must add a very thin line of highlight above your new line so that it looks natural. You will notice that everyone has a natural highlight above the top lip and if you fail to add this to the newly defined lip, the new lip will look artificial and flat. If you have a wide mouth, do not bring the lip liner all the way into the corners of the mouth. Allow the liner to alter your lips if necessary. A slight uplift to the line can give a turned down mouth a more natural shape. Outline the lips with a slightly deeper pencil than the lipstick; they need not match exactly. For best results, apply the lipstick with a lip brush, as the color tends to stay truer and last longer. Blotting the lips with a tissue helps the staying power and gives a matte finish. However, if you would like, a little gloss or even a little highlight in the center of the bottom lip can add a nice fullness to the lips. If you have very full lips and want them to appear a bit smaller, create a new line on the inside of the lips and add foundation to the outer area of the lips.

ROUGE (BLUSH)

Blush is one of the final touches to give emphasis to the face and can serve as a contour, highlight, or both. Powder blush is preferable, and the color should flatter your face as well as complement the costume. If you have applied shadow and highlight to your cheeks, you will now want to add blush to blend the two.

Using a blush brush, follow the same shape as your shadow, lightly blending the edges so that the blush does not leave a harsh line. (Often, if you just happen to have the right shape face and the right color blush, this step is what is used for the shadow, as illustrated in Figures 8.1 and 8.2.) Next, fade your blush color into the highlight on top of your cheekbone. What you should notice is that the contour of your cheek still has the dimensional look of high cheekbones but now appears to be blended and subtle. Be careful that the blush is not placed too close to the eyes or nose. To even out or balance the face, add a light touch of blush around the hairline, around the jawline, and on the bottom of the chin. To complete the look, tap off excess blush and lightly dust the blush brush over your entire eye and eyebrow area. If you have added too much blush anywhere on your face, you can tone it down with a little foundation or powder. However, to avoid this problem altogether, it is wise to use your hand as a palette: take the brush and gently tap it into the makeup, then dust off the excess on your hand before applying it to your face. A good blush brush will be an invaluable addition to your makeup kit, both for personal and theatrical use.

MAKEUP FOR MEN

Although not significantly different in concept, it is the application and amount of makeup that is different for men and women. Therefore, men should use the information in the entire chapter and modify their makeup accordingly. Men generally have heavier eyebrows and brow bones than do women; thus highlight is placed only on the eyelid (over the eyeball area) and lightly shadowed at the crease to give it depth. The eyes are lined at the lashes, although not as dramatically as with women. The nose should be contoured to flatter the dancer, and a little shadow added under the cheek to add dimension from the stage. Shadowing at the jawline should be stronger for the male. Remember to add a little highlight above the shadow contour (at the cheek and jawline), and then lightly add blush (*not* pink) to even out the color. Men do not contour with blush but rather dust the face with color, giving a touch more to the cheeks than to the rest of the face. Excess makeup may be removed with a tissue. If you are not using full body makeup and are not adding extra makeup to your hands as a matter of course, you may want to add blush color lightly across your knuckles so that when your hands come close to your made up face, there is not such an obvious difference.

HAIR

Traditionally, hair for the female dancer has been pulled back tightly from the face and rolled into the proverbial bun, and for good reason: the hair is out of the face and not a distraction to the dancer or the audience. This principle can still hold true for contemporary dance but does not need to be limited to such conventional fashion. The important element of hair-styling for dance is to keep it from becoming the focus (unless, of course, it is intended to be). There are as many methods and styles as can be imagined to accomplish this end, and the completed hair style will naturally depend on your own hair and/or the design concept. Long hair can be contained in many flattering styles but still left loose and flowing; short hair, too, can be slicked or fashionably contained so that it does not interfere with the dancer. Hair accessories (e.g., barrettes, combs, or bands that complement the costume or concept) can be used to enhance your hairdo as well as functionally serve in the styling of a particular look that can keep your hair out of your eyes. You will inevitably also need a lot of bobby pins, hair gel, and hair spray.

Whenever possible, it is desirable to use your own hair, as it is one less variable to consider. If for any number of reasons an added hairpiece is called for, it is important to know how to attach it to your hair. Basically, the process for anchoring hairpieces is the same for most types (e.g., falls, braids, ponytails, wiglets).

Once you have decided where to position the hairpiece on your head, part your hair at that spot; then, comb the front hair forward and clip it to get it temporarily out of the way. At the part, take small segments of your hair and make flat pin curls with bobby pins that crisscross. Generally, a small row of two to three pin curls close together is sufficient. Most hairpieces come with a comb attached inside at the top and center; you will use this comb to anchor the hairpiece by slipping it into the pin curls. Put the comb just in front of and slightly gripping the pin curls, and push the teeth of the comb into the pin curls securely (small combs may grab only one pin curl).

Once the hairpiece is attached at its center, anchor it more securely by pinning it into your own hair with bobby pins. You may need to secure the hairpiece with pins in various other places as well. Now, remove the clip that you used to temporarily section off the portion of your own hair in front of the hairpiece and brush this hair back into the hairpiece to blend the two together. Take as many opportunities as you can to pin your own hair into the hairpiece for added security and to hide any edges of the hairpiece.

Remember that you must match the color of the hairpiece to your own hair very carefully, so that in the blending process there really will be no noticeable difference between the artificial hair and your own. Naturally, whatever it takes to anchor a hairpiece securely is what you need to do. If five bobby pins securely hold the piece on, use ten for a dance.

CONCLUSION

The bottom line on makeup is: Does it work? Keep in mind what you are trying to accomplish. Can you be seen from the balcony? Have the shadows and highlights created enough depth to the natural contours of the face so that you do not appear flat, but at the same time do not look like you are covered with war paint? Have you maintained the theatricality and integrity of the traditional art form? If you are in an ensemble piece, is your makeup consistent with the other members of the ensemble? Trust that during the technical and dress rehearsals somebody is looking at you from the house and can best answer these questions for you. Remember that what looks extreme in the mirror to you may be the perfect balance under the lights on the stage. Eventually, you will trust what you have done and become comfortable knowing what will look best on you. Remember that makeup, like dance, takes work. The more you practice, the better you become.

SOURCES

- Bob Kelly, 1515 West 46th Street, New York, NY 10036
- Kryolan, 745 Polk Street, San Francisco, CA 94109
- Mehron, 100 Red Schoolhouse Rd., Chestnut Ridge, NY 10977
- Ben Nye, 5935 Bowcroft Street, Los Angeles, CA 90016

9 . Box Office and House Management

PAUL STUART GRAHAM   *Faculty, Department of Theatre Arts, California State University, Long Beach. Managing Director, California Repertory Company.*

RONALD ALLAN-LINDBLOM   *Faculty, Department of Theatre Arts, California State University, Long Beach. Associate Artistic Producing Director, California Repertory Company.*

THE BOX OFFICE

A box office, by definition, refers to an office where tickets of admission are sold. It is, moreover, the "lifeline" of a theatre. It must be well organized and managed in order for it to function effectively. The box office is typically managed and organized by the box-office manager. If there is no box-office manager, it is managed by the theatre's personnel, and the dance concert director should be able to rely on their expertise to supervise box-office procedures. The box office should also be regarded as the beginning of the theatregoing experience. The image of the theatre and the personnel who work in it should reinforce public confidence. Accuracy, detail, and friendliness are important factors in attracting new customers to the performing arts.

Location

Ideally, the box office should be easily accessible to the public and part of the theatre structure. It should be clearly marked and recognizable as a ticket office. The box-office window or service counter should be located so that it does not obstruct the public going to or from the theatre at performance times. It is usually a good idea for the box office to be located close to the theatre's patron parking area. Availability of parking for walk-up patrons is a major advantage in attracting patrons to purchase tickets in advance.

When the theatre is located a distance from the local business district or does not sell seats to walk-up patrons in advance, satellite box-office locations should be considered. Many patrons will purchase tickets at stores and ticket agencies.

Equipment

The following types of equipment will facilitate the running of an efficient box office.

Ticket racks. These have become an obsolete fixture in most box offices. However, if the box-office operation does not have a computerized ticket-printing machine, it may be necessary to construct a built-in ticket rack or purchase a portable rack. Most ticket-printing companies sell, for a modest price, portable ticket racks that accommodate a number of tickets and can be locked.

Cash registers or cash drawer. These should be located so that the box-office attendant can make change without turning away from the customer. Cash registers or cash drawers should have keys and should be locked when not in use. There are a number of cash register models available. Select the register that best fits the needs of the operation. Depending on the number of people involved in the box office and the cash systems that are used, it may be best to purchase a register that allows for more than one attendant to work out of it. This eliminates the need for separate drawers and expedites closing out the box office.

Adding machines. These are primarily used to compute box-office statements and bank deposits.

Safes. The safe should be located in the box-office area and should be out of view of the public. It should be fireproof and made immobile. The box office should never store large amounts of cash in its safe. The safe should be used *only* to hold box-office receipts on a temporary basis between scheduled bank deposits.

Credit card machines. Most box-office ticket sales are credit card sales. Box-office attendants should be familiar with the use of imprinters and machines designed to authorize charge sales.

Computerized ticket equipment. Most box offices use a computerized system to generate tickets and to audit ticket sales. These systems have been designed to simplify the point of sale activity and have greatly reduced the time needed to accommodate the customer at the service counter. Computerized systems are an expensive investment but are becoming an increasingly necessary box-office fixture.

Word processors and typewriters. All box-office business correspondence, records, and reports should be made on a word processor or typewriter; handwriting may be illegible. Uniformity of correspondence and recording greatly assists the box-office manager in accurately reporting box-office activity.

Telephones. Choosing the right telephone system for your box-office operation is extremely important. Too often, box-office operations do not allow for enough telephone lines or for a rollover system that transfers incoming calls to another line. When only one telephone line is available, the customer cannot get through quickly to purchase tickets and becomes frustrated. Remember that the theatregoing experience begins at the box office. The customer call needs to be answered in a timely fashion. An answering device should be used when the office is closed. The information to the caller should be brief. There is nothing more aggravating than having to listen to unnecessary information particularly when the customer is paying for the call.

Security

Complete security is required for the storage of tickets and cash. The installation of a burglar system provides good protection and often deters intruders from entering the box office when it is closed.

Internal security is also an important consideration when dealing with personnel and cash. All too often internal theft takes place when cash is present. Management should implement a variety of procedures to discourage personnel from attempting to short the cash register. The procedure of having two signatures on daily box-office reconciliation reports is a good practice, and quite often keeps everyone honest when reporting cash sales.

Personnel

The box-office attendant is usually the first contact that the customer has with the dance event. The attendant is the ambassador for the theatre and has a responsibility to ensure that the theatregoer has a positive experience. Box-office attendants should be efficient and courteous and have a knowledge of, or at the very least, an interest in what is being sold. An operational manual describing employee responsibilities and duties, and customer relation policy (Figure 9.1) should be available in the box office.

CUSTOMER SERVICE GUIDELINES

Our customer service guidelines are simple. We want a win/win resolution. This involves a collaborative effort between the patron and cashier or box office manager. We value our customers and strive to understand what it is they are saying. Never tell customers that they are wrong. Explore constructive alternatives, value differences of opinion and seek objective feedback. Sometimes a customer just wants a refund and nothing else will suffice. Often times, giving them a name and address where they may express their displeasure about a performance is all they want.

You can do a lot toward de-escalating a situation or at least setting an atmosphere so that a supervisor may engage in a non-combative discussion

(1) Listen to what the customer is saying.
    Listen empathetically to others.
    Stop yourself from working on counter-arguments while customers are speaking.
    Keep your anger and emotions out of the interaction.
    Risk being persuaded by what the customer is saying.
    Don't assume you know how they feel.
    Stand inside their shoes for a minute.

(2) Ask for complete details of the complaint.
    Make sure you understand the problem.
    Restate the person's basic idea, emphasizing facts.
    Restate your understanding of the customer's complaint.

(3) Evaluate the situation and consider your options.
    Involve customers in solving problems. i.e. "How would you like this problem to be solved?"

(4) Don't attack the customer.
    You may disagree with unrealistic solutions but don't interrupt.
    Be open, specific, honest and direct in your discourse.
    Sarcasm is inappropriate.

(5) Stay calm.
    Try to reach an agreement on how the complaint will be handled.
    Summarize what has happened.
    Thank the customer for bringing the complaint/concern to your attention.

The 5 pitfalls of handling complaints:
    Taking the complaint personally. (They are not angry at you.)
    Interrupting the customer. (Let them blow off steam.)
    Sounding like a recording.
    Arguing with the customer.
    Blaming the problem on equipment, other departments, or other employees.

Figure 9.1 Customer service guidelines.

Figure 9.2 Ticket, front and back.

THE TICKET

A ticket (Figure 9.2) is a token showing that an admission fee has been paid. It represents a legal agreement between the theatre and the patron to honor what is printed on the ticket. The patron assumes that the information printed on the ticket is true, correct, and will actually take place. Should the event not take place as printed on the ticket, the theatre has the responsibility to refund the patron the total cost of the ticket. The theatre may suggest that patrons exchange their tickets for an alternate date, but it cannot demand that customers do so. If the theatre is not sure of its programming, which is often the case with performing arts centers that offer a series of productions, it may be best to add the phrase "programs subject to change" on the printed ticket. This policy allows the management more flexibility when offering ticket refunds and exchanges. The phrase "no refunds or exchanges" printed on the ticket is another option.

Ordering tickets

Most box-office operations are equipped with computerized ticket-printing machines. However, if your box office is not equipped with such a machine you will need to order tickets from a ticket-printing company. There are two basic types of tickets, the reserved and the nonreserved, or general admission, ticket.

The *reserved ticket* requires more information printed on the ticket than the nonreserved ticket, and therefore is more expensive. Most reserved tickets require the following information:

- Title of the production
- Performance date
- Curtain time
- Name of the theatre
- Section (orchestra, balcony, mezzanine, etc.)
- Seat number
- Row number
- Price of the ticket
- Telephone number of the box office

When ordering reserved tickets, consider the kind of audit stub desired. Audit stubs are used to determine the exact sales for each event. All vital information should appear on the ticket and the stub so that patrons can find their seats and the box office can conduct a proper accounting of each ticket sale.

Tickets should be printed in different colors when (1) the theatre is scaled (different-priced seats may be different colors) and (2) a single ticket price is used for a large theatre and different sections of the theatre are given different colored tickets to quickly direct patrons to their seats.

The theatre should provide a seating chart (Figure 9.3) showing the exact number and arrangement of all seats in the theatre. The floor plan should clearly show every seat, indicating seat number, row, section, and aisles. This floor plan or document is referred to as a ticket manifest.

The *nonreserved ticket* may be similar to the reserved ticket in that much of the same information is required, but the portion pertaining

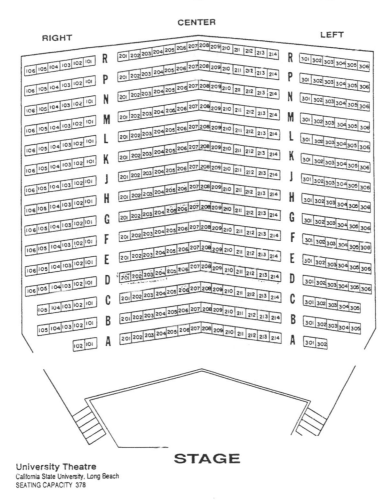

Figure 9.3 Theatre seating chart or ticket manifest.

to the seat location is eliminated. A second type is simpler and may be ordered in roll form, like those used by movie theatres. It has no information printed on the ticket but is numbered in order to conduct a proper accounting.

Computerized tickets

Not to be confused with computerized box-office systems are tickets that are printed in bulk by computers. Many ticket-printing companies make it possible to order and deliver computer-printed tickets at very short notice and for a relatively low price.

Selling tickets

Selling tickets involves careful preparation. There are several tasks that are routinely done prior to opening the box office. Although the process may differ from one theatre to the next, the one factor that remains constant is careful attention to detail. Selling tickets is an exacting business; there is no room for error. Knowing the procedures and policies for selling tickets can eliminate costly mistakes.

If the box office does not use a computerized system, the first task is racking the tickets. This needs to be done in a meticulous fashion, and should be checked by another person to prevent mistakes. The person so designated should "pull" tickets for special purposes for every performance. These may be:

- House seats (these seats are held by the box office for emergency use or for a specific need)
- Press seats (for opening-night critics and other performances as needed)
- Complimentary seats, or "comps" (for cast and crew members, VIPs, or others)
- Dead seats (seats that may not be sold because they have been removed or have an obstructed view)

Special passes, special discount vouchers, and any other type of complimentary tickets are referred to as "hardwood." Typically, passes are exchanged at the box office for tickets.

Once the necessary season subscriber series, group sales, press, and house seats have been removed, tickets should be sold on a first-come, first-served basis. Most people attending theatre are not familiar enough with the layout of a theatre to know where the best seats are. Box-office attendants should be familiar with the seating configuration. The box-office attendant must be patient and courteous when discussing seating availability.

Taking reservations

Taking ticket reservations can be time-consuming. However, this has been made easier through computerized telephone and credit card purchases. Theatregoers pick the seating section according to price, and the computer chooses the best available seat. If your organization does not have a computerized ticket system the attendant will have to require patrons to claim and pay for their tickets in

```
CALIFORNIA STATE UNIVERSITY, LONG BEACH
RICHARD AND KAREN CARPENTER PERFORMING ARTS CENTER
COLLEGE OF THE ARTS

PATRON:_____    EVENT:_____
         LAST NAME          INITIAL
PHONE:_____    TIME:_____  DATE:_____

NOTES:_____    NUMBER OF TICKETS:_____

_____     COMP:__ PREPAID:__ COD:$_____

ARTS TICKET OFFICE
6200 ATHERTON STREET · LONG BEACH, CA 90815
TELEPHONE: 310/985-7000 · FAX: 310/985-7023 · TDD: 310/985-7097

THANK YOU FOR YOUR PATRONAGE!
```

Figure 9.4 Ticket envelope.

advance of the production. As a rule ten percent of all theatre tickets will not be claimed. The box office should, therefore, keep unpaid reservations to a minimum.

Ticket envelopes (Figure 9.4), which hold the ticket, should have all the necessary reservation information. Theatres should order preprinted envelopes to ensure that box-office attendants do not omit any of the crucial reservation information.

Telephone reservations

Box-office telephones need to be answered promptly. These phones should not be used for private calls. If telephone lines are frequently busy, the customer will get discouraged and choose not to obtain tickets or information. A box-office ticket order form (Figure 9.5) can suggest a specific procedure for obtaining the required reservation information. Transactions should be brief but clear.

Group sales

Many theatres offer to organizations group discounts of ten to fifty percent off the regular ticket price. A binding contract should be drawn up between the theatre and the organization purchasing the block of tickets. No ticket should be released without full payment.

Season subscriptions

Season subscriptions are a good strategy for selling tickets. Subscribers get the best seats at the best prices, sometimes up to fifty

CENTRAL TICKET OFFICE - TICKET ORDER FORM

PATRON NAME:_____ CUST. #:_____ DATE OF ORDER:_____
ADDRESS:_____ ORDER TAKEN BY:_____
CITY:_____ ZIP CODE:_____ REFUND/EXCH. INFO.: _____
HOME PHONE:_____ WORK PHONE:_____ FAX:_____
VISA/MC ACCT:_____ EXP:_____ AUTH #:_____

EVENT	DAY	DATE	TIME	QTY	PRICE	TOTAL	VENUE	# EVENT	SEAT LOCATION/INFO

| SERVICE CHARGE | | | 3.00 | TIX IN W/C DATE:_____ |

ORDER TOTAL $ _____   TIX MAILED DATE:_____
                           BY:_____

BE SURE TO REPEAT ENTIRE ORDER TO PATRON TO VERIFY ACCURACY!

Figure 9.5 Ticket order form.

percent savings over single admissions. Other benefits may include free or reduced-rate parking, ticket exchanges, and pre- and post-show restaurant discounts.

Special discounts

Student and senior citizen discounts, pay-what-you-can performances, twofers (two for the cost of one ticket), and rush tickets (unsold tickets put on sale at greatly reduced prices just prior to the performance) are some of the many special incentives offered by theatres to generate ticket sales.

Dressing and papering the house

When it appears that a performance is not selling out, the box-office manager can "dress the house" by scattering the customers throughout each section of the theatre. This gives the illusion of a much larger audience than is actually in attendance.

When ticket sales are going poorly, free tickets are often distributed to individuals and/or organizations in order to help fill the theatre. However, this "papering the house" policy can create problems. It establishes a word of mouth that business is bad and, therefore, the production must be bad. Others feel that giving away tickets will reduce the number of paying customers.

COLLEGE OF THE ARTS TICKET OFFICE
PERFORMANCE DATE SALES REPORT

PERFORMANCE INFORMATION

EVENT:_____

DAY/DATE:_____ TIME:_____

VENUE:_____

TICKETS DISTRIBUTED:

COMPS ....: _____ @   N/C

GENERAL ....: _____ @ $ _____ = $ _____

DISCOUNT ....: _____ @ $ _____ = $ _____

_____: _____ @ $ _____ = $ _____

_____: _____ @ $ _____ = $ _____

_____: _____ @ $ _____ = $ _____

TOTALS ....: _____ $ _____

METHOD OF PAYMENT:

CASH ....: $ _____

CHECKS ....: $ _____

CHARGES ....: $ _____

_____: $ _____

_____: $ _____

_____: $ _____

❬ THESE MUST AGREE ❭ $ _____

TIME BOX OFFICE OPENED: _____

TIME BOX OFFICE CLOSED: _____

HOUSE STAFF PRESENT: HOUSE MANAGER: _____   TICKET TAKER: _____   USHERS: _____

NOTES TO CASHIER:_____

_____

_____

_____

_____

CASHIER COMMENTS: _____

_____

_____

_____

_____

_____

CASHIER:_____   SIGNATURE:_____

Figure 9.6 Box-office statement/sales report.

Papering the house (distributing free tickets) may be a good idea at times. It can greatly increase the visibility of a production. Most theatres routinely give away complimentary tickets to members of the press and to patrons who support the organization. However, papering the house should be done sparingly and judiciously.

BOX-OFFICE ACCOUNTING

Each theatre needs to establish an accounting of tickets sold. The procedure for auditing will vary depending on the sophistication of the box office. A computerized system will make the task of accounting for tickets easier and quicker. Whatever the type operation, the box-office attendant must account for every ticket sold.

A daily box-office statement (Figure 9.6) should provide information such as the event, date, number of tickets distributed in each category (including comps, season, and discounted), and revenue generated. If the organization honors credit cards for ticket purchases, this information will also be reported on the daily sales report.

Tickets that have not been sold for an event are called "deadwood." These tickets are counted. The difference between the number of tickets available for sale and the deadwood should equal the number of tickets sold plus the comps. Audit stubs should correspond with this number. If there is an error, all tickets should be recounted.

After the statement has been finalized, the stubs and deadwood should be stored in a safe place for at least three years for tax reporting purposes.

HOUSE MANAGEMENT

House management is a critical component of any production because it deals with the most important aspect of the event: the patrons. For patrons the experience begins with their arrival at the theatre. How they are treated before, during, and after the performance influences their perception of the production.

In the same way that the stage manager is responsible for the running of the production, the house manager is responsible for the safety and comfort of the audience.

Communication among production personnel

The house manager works closely with the stage manager and the box-office manager. Most theatres have an intercom system that allows these three to communicate quickly and efficiently. In order for the performance to begin at the publicized time, house management, stage management, and box-office management must be in harmony. The house manager will give the final "go" to the stage manager to begin the performance. If there are any problems that call for the curtain time to be delayed, the house manager must be notified of the situation.

Example: Two-thirds of tonight's audience is comprised of a group sale to an organization arriving in buses. Ten minutes before curtain the box office receives a call saying that the buses are stuck in traffic and will be arriving ten or fifteen minutes after the performance is scheduled to begin. What do you do? Hold the curtain? Begin the production knowing that the performance will be disrupted by the late seating of the majority of the audience? The house manager must make this decision and communicate to all areas how to proceed. Without constant and clear communication with the box office and the stage manager a brilliant production could be compromised.

Emergency procedures

The house manager and house management staff are responsible for the safety of the audience. The house manager should know emergency procedures and how to respond to specific situations, and is required to make certain that the house management staff is familiar with the theatre's prescribed emergency policies and procedures. In the unlikely case of any catastrophic event the house manager and his or her staff must evacuate the audience safely and effectively. Theatres and presenting houses are required by law to have published guidelines showing evacuation routes and stating emergency procedures. It is imperative that the house manager and house management staff are prepared and knowledgeable.

Supervision of house management staff

In the ideal world ushers, ticket takers, and cloakroom attendants are all paid positions hired by the house manager. This may be true of large presenting houses but is rarely the case in smaller ones. Often, the ushers and ticket takers are volunteers and this labor pool changes from performance to performance. It is therefore important for the house manager to provide written instructions and procedures to the house management staff prior to the event. Seating procedures, ticket-taking requirements, dress code policies, and call times should be provided to the staff in advance.

In addition, the house manager should call the staff together at least thirty minutes before the house is to open to review the following:

- Emergency procedures
- Ticket taking
- Seating policies

- Program information
- Intermission procedures
- Theatre policies (food, drinks, smoking)
- Late-seating procedures
- Post-show procedures

House manager's report

The purpose of this report is to provide a record of the house management of a specific performance. The report is useful to key production personnel who may not have been in attendance. Producers, business managers, and publicists can often gauge information about a specific evening based on this report. The report also serves as a checklist the house manager can use to ensure that the theatre and its staff are prepared for the upcoming performance. The report is completed nightly by the house manager and turned in to the business manager for distribution. It is the responsibility of the house manager to complete and sign this report after each performance. (Figure 9.7)

SUMMARY

Safety, comfort, and efficiency are the goals of house management. The fact that we use the word "house" to represent the theatre tells us that patrons are guests coming into our home. They should be treated as such if we wish them to return. Patrons may forgive a bad performance but not a bad experience. They will return to a house that makes them feel welcome, secure, and appreciated.

CALIFORNIA REPERTORY COMPANY
1250 BELLFLOWER BLVD.
LONG BEACH, CA. 90840

HOUSE MANAGEMENT REPORT

Production_____

Date_____ Time_____

House Manager_____ Phone_____

Box Office Manager_____ Phone_____

Ushers_____ Ticket Taker_____
_____   _____
_____   _____
_____
_____

TO BE COMPLETED BY THE HOUSE MANAGER

Start Time_____ Intermission begin time_____
                          Intermission end time_____

Weather_____Parking conditions_____

Box Office problems_____

Head Count_____ Stub Count_____ Usher Count_____

Remarks_____
_____
_____

House Manager Signature_____ Date_____

Figure 9.7 House management report.

10 . Marketing

SAM DAWSON   *Program officer for the Ahmanson Foundation, a philanthropic agency in Los Angeles. Owner of a public-relations firm specializing in the arts for twenty-five years.*

How do you get the word out and how do you position your dance company so that people are aware of it, know it is good, want to attend concerts, and want to support the company? The answer: market your product. That means using all available tools to reach your potential audience and supporters.

Where do you find these people? There is the general public, the dance community, theatregoers, students, senior citizens, and those who go to other dance events. You may come up with others. You need to analyze and target just who would enjoy your performance. For example, senior citizens are a potential group because they have the time, the expendable income, and the interest. Once you decide on your various publics, develop a plan to reach them.

First consider how to structure your dance company. If you are on a high school or college campus, you have the luxury of using the nonprofit status of that educational institution. When you form your own company you must decide if it is a for-profit or a nonprofit organization. Although "for-profit" sounds better, the most common and practical way to structure your dance company is as a not-for-profit, tax-exempt corporation, which is a 501 (C)3 organization. This status has many practical applications, ranging from tax advantages to raising deductible donations (fundraising) to taking advantage of public service announcements (PSAs) which are free advertisements on radio and television.

As a nonprofit organization with a solid board committed to your artistic mission, you now need to work out a budget that includes adequate funding for marketing. Once you have done so, you can begin a campaign to let people know you exist.

If you do not qualify for nonprofit status immediately, a possible first step is to affiliate with a group that already has a 501 (C)3.

GETTING ORGANIZED

The very first thing is to create a timeline of tasks to ensure that the concert gets the best possible exposure and the most people to come. You need to begin your marketing campaign at least three to four months prior to the event.

A full-blown marketing campaign includes a budget for both advertising and publicity. The difference between them is sometimes confusing but, in fact, it is very simple: you pay to buy advertising space; publicity is free. Advertising is expensive to create and to place. To give you an idea, an ad in a major metropolitan newspaper that is two columns wide and three inches high costs thousands of dollars; buying air time on radio costs hundreds of dollars for a thirty-second spot and even more on television. This does not include the cost of producing the print ads or the radio or television spots. New dance companies and student groups seldom, if ever, have an advertising budget. Happily, a well-thought-out marketing campaign can still be successful without one.

PRINT MEDIA

Press releases

Press releases are the backbone of marketing and they have a standard format. Although it is best to use plain white paper, letterhead is often used. In the upper right-hand corner put the release date or "FOR IMMEDIATE RELEASE" along with the current date. Seldom will you send a release that you want held, so nine times out of ten you will put "FOR IMMEDIATE RELEASE." In the upper left-hand corner, put the company name and address and the "contact" person (which is usually you) with a telephone number. This is extremely important. If a reporter has a question a quick response will be required, so make sure to use a telephone number where you are readily available. When you speak to the press, be honest; even if you would rather not tell the reporter something it is best to be candid. For the most part, reporters will be understanding. Honesty will always pay off. If a reporter knows you can be trusted, you will build a good relationship and nothing is more important for you and your company or school.

Back to the format. Always double space your copy. At the end of the first page, type "more" if you are to continue. When the release

Contact: Sam Dawson
The Hot Shot Dance Company   November 8, 1998
(310) 765-4321   FOR IMMEDIATE RELEASE

THE HOT SHOT DANCE COMPANY TO PERFORM AT CITY THEATRE, SEPTEMBER 23–OCTOBER 5

The Hot Shot Dance company will open Tuesday, September 23rd at City Theatre, 2424 East Street, Anywhere, for a two week run. The company, called "an American treasure" by President Clinton, will be premiering "Jazz Ditty" choreographed by the company's director Bill Smith. Opening night will also feature Smith's signature piece, "Too Hot for Hot Shots," as well as the highly acclaimed "Ring of Flame." That program will be repeated Saturday evenings, September 27 and October 1, Tuesday evening, October 30, and Sunday matinees September 28 and October 5. "Crazy Baby," "Blue Too Too," and "Ain't Happy," a dance critics have called powerful and dynamic, will be performed on Wednesday evenings, September 24 and October 1, and Sunday evenings, September 28 and October 5. The full length "Bodies Beautiful" will be presented in only two performances, Thursday evenings September 25 and October 2. *Time Magazine* touted "Bodies Beautiful" as "the most stunning, lyrical and magical dance to be created by any choreographer since Balanchine."

Bill Smith and his Hot Shot Company, now in their fifth season, have played to sold out audiences world wide.

Ticket prices range from $15 to $50. For information and ticket reservations call (310) 123-4567.

###

Figure 10.1 Sample press release.

has ended, put -30- or ### to indicate that it is the end of the release. When writing put all the most important facts first and less essential information later in the story. There is an old rule in journalism called the four Ws and an H: who, what, when, where, and how. Answer as many of these questions as you can and get the facts in the first or second paragraph. Always be precise and accurate. Spelling counts. Check and double-check. Do not depend on "spell check" on your computer; it will not pick up things such as "form" for "from" or "dancer" for "dancers."

Say it simply. Do not use long run-on sentences with lots of commas. Be clear, simple, precise, and accurate. It would be wise to invest in the *Associated Press Style Book,* which can be found in any good bookstore or local library. Remember, the press release (Figure 10.1) is your basic information tool and you want to put your very best face on it.

Your first press release most likely will be your season release, so there will be many facts to cover, including dancers' names and the names of music and composers. Take your time and do it well. Then, have someone else look at it for accuracy. It is difficult to find your own mistakes.

Not only is there the season release, but also each dance concert will need its own release. Make sure that all ticket and contact information is correct and included. The season release should be sent out to monthly magazines at least three months in advance. Along with the season release, you may also send captioned photographs if the magazine uses such things. You may also indicate that color slides are available upon request, if, of course, you have color. The information about color slides should be on a separate sheet of paper in memo form, for example:

To: The Editor
Fr: You
Re: Color Slides

FYI color slides are available upon request.

Press kits

The press kit is your most important ongoing marketing tool. It is distributed to media, interested potential funders, and anyone else who needs an in-depth look at your company. It should include most or all of the following materials: a season release; a company history; a fact sheet; photographs with captions; bios on the dancers; a copy of the season brochure, if appropriate; and reprints of any news articles on the company, again, if appropriate. For best results, the press kit should be prepared at least three to four months in advance of opening. Once you have compiled all the appropriate information, you are pretty well prepared for any and all media inquiries.

Fact sheets are like a press release, except that the information is laid out with "just the facts." A good format is to list who, what, where, and when. It is a handy tool in that it gives concise information at a glance. The fact sheet will often be included with a "pitch letter" (see *Feature Stories*, below) or with other general information you may be sending out. As you go through this chapter, fact sheet uses will become apparent.

Photographs, particularly in dance, are a must. In general they should be 8″ × 10″ black and white. Generally, newspapers will reject color photos. Color slides are wonderful to have on hand for brochures and magazines. Occasionally, some weeklies and daily newspapers will also request them. The ideal photographs are action photographs. Posed photographs are seldom, if ever, used. Getting a good action photograph is not an easy job. Sports photographers are accustomed to action; if you can afford it, call your local newspaper sports desk and engage one of their photographers. Your local college newspaper is another possibility. A good student photographer is more likely to fit your budget.

Photograph captions are important. They are "mini press releases" and should include the contact name and telephone number. They must be double spaced, identify the dancers (always from left to right), and include crucial facts about the performance, including the ticket information. It is possible that a photograph may run without your entire press release, so it is important to include the basic information even if you feel you are repeating yourself. The caption should be securely taped to the back of the photograph. Never attach anything to the front, as it will make the photograph unusable. A good way to attach a caption is to write it about halfway down the page, tape the page to the back, and fold the page around the photo. When the editor looks at the photograph, the caption will be at the bottom and attached at the back.

Cast biographies (bios) can be a good source for publicity. Cast members should be required to fill out a sheet on themselves for your marketing files (Figure 10.2). That information can be used in

---

Bio Form

Name:
Address:
City:
Phone: Home: Work: Pager:

Education to date:

What dances do you perform?

Do you have reviews? (If so, do you have copies? Please supply.)

Previous dance experience:

Do you have other theatre arts experience besides dance? List:

What experience or jobs do you have outside of dance?

What are your hobbies?

List your awards and/or affiliations:

If you have a resume, please attach.

Please add anything you like. Use the back of this form and additional paper if necessary.

Figure 10.2 Dancer bio form.

the program and may be handy for a story angle (see *Feature Stories,* below).

The season brochure is a very important marketing tool. It will be the most costly item in your budget but your best sales piece and your company's most important monetary investment. You will need a good photographer, well-written copy, and the talent of a good graphic designer. Today's desk-top publishing makes simple brochures much easier to create. Even so, you need a design that is eye-catching, easy to read, and compelling, in short, a promotional piece that will make people read it and then subscribe for a season.

Press list

Your press list should be compiled well in advance, with great care, and updated on a regular basis. Get your information from the library, from other arts organizations, and from places that deal in media lists, such as the Public Communicators of Los Angeles and Southern California's Broadcasters Association. (See Figure 10.3.)

The press list should include all appropriate outlets, including magazines, weekly newspapers, daily newspapers, ethnic papers, throwaways, radio and television stations, and freelance writers. At newspapers you may have several people on your list, such as the dance critic, a feature writer, and the society editor. There also may be several people at radio and television stations on your list. Freelance writers looking for a good story to sell to a magazine or a newspaper are good to have on the list as well. When you create your list, include pertinent data such as deadlines and special interests of editors. As time goes by, your list will grow. It is important that you read the publications, listen to radio, and watch television shows that might be an appropriate outlet for dance company publicity. An important note: *do not address press releases to "editor" or "dance editor."* Call and get a name and be sure that you spell it correctly.

Other publicity and advertising

Calendar listings are another way to get exposure. Many magazines and newspapers use them. It is important for you to follow the format required and mail in the listing by the deadline. Again, magazines need material months in advance, and newspapers usually need material at least three weeks prior to an event.

Feature stories are articles you read about a dance company, for the most part in the arts and leisure section of a newspaper. Have you wondered how a story like that happened to appear? The answer is that a good publicist thought of an "angle" and "pitched" the idea to a reporter or a freelance writer who, in turn, "sold" the idea to the newspaper. Dreaming up ideas and pitching them to both

Radio Stations

Station/Format	Contact	Lengths Accepted		Live Copy	Tape
KABC/KTZN (Talk) P.O. Box 790 Los Angeles 90016 Attn: PSA	Nelkane Benton (310) 840-4915	30	60	x	x

Send material 6-8 weeks prior to desired air date. Tape for 30 or 60-second only, on reel or CD.

KACE (Urban) 610 S. Ardmore Los Angeles 90005	Patricia Means (213) 427-7915 FAX (213) 380-4214	30	x

Submit material 2-3 weeks prior to desired air date.

KACD/KBCD (Hot AC) 1425 Fifth St. Santa Monica 90401	John Darrell (310) 458-1031 FAX(310) 393-2443	2 0	x

Material must be received 3 weeks in advance of air date. Live copy only.

NOTE: Please do not contact general managers or news directors regarding Public Service Announcements. Deal only with the Public Service Director.

Television Stations

Slides submitted to stations: Please identify slides with name of organization (also include address and/or phone number). Slides concernng special events should include dates of the events.

Station	Contact	Requirements
KABC-TV (Channel 7) 4151 Prospect Ave. Los Angeles 90027	Teresa Samaniego (310) 557-4720	1" tapes in 10, 15, 20, 30 or 60 second spots. No slides accepted. Material must be dated and at station 6 weeks before air time. Include copy of script and proof of non-profit status.
KCAL-TV (Channel 9) 5515 Melrose Ave Hollywood 90038 Attn: Public Affairs Dept.	Martin Quiroz (213) 960-3688	Beta SP tapes in 10, 15, 20, 30 and 60 second spots. Live copy also accepted for community calendar. No slides. Send proof of non-profit status. Local spots take precedence.

Figure 10.3 Extracts from a Southern California Broadcasters Association listing for radio and television.

print and broadcast media will create the very best media attention you can get.

You know your company, you know your choreography and you know your dancers. Similar to staging an event, you need to create legitimate and interesting story angles to be pitched. A good source of ideas will come from the company bios. The pitch may be on a dancer who, in early childhood, was told he would never walk again. It may be about a choreographer who grew up in the inner city and was a gang member. It may be about how your company was born and what makes it different from any other dance company. Again, use your creative abilities. Once you have a few story angles, write a pitch letter and send it to your media contact or, if it is a particularly visual story, to a television news or interview show. With radio, you would want to pitch an idea that could be discussed on the air, such as an interview with the ex-gang-member choreographer.

After you write to the appropriate media person, you then follow up the pitch letter. You can never just mail the pitch and call it a day. You must follow up with a call. As mentioned earlier, it is your second chance to sell the idea. When you call the media, always ask if they are on deadline. If they are, ask when it might be convenient for you to call again. Reporters do not want to deal with you when they are fighting a deadline. If they turn you down, be polite and thank them for their time. The most important thing is to establish good rapport. You want the press to be your friend. They have control over the distribution of your information and if they think of you as a polite professional, they will be more likely to give consideration to your ideas.

Exchanging tickets for free advertising space is another possibility. Sometimes weekly newspapers will take a block of tickets in exchange for an ad that would otherwise cost you money. Your tickets are often the best barter you have and, in the long run, less expensive than paying for advertising space or air time.

BROADCAST MEDIA

Public service announcements (PSAs)

These are free advertisements on radio and television for your organization. Radio and television stations are required by law to make free air time available to qualified nonprofit organizations. PSAs are a good way to get exposure on the airwaves, but you must remember that there is great competition for free air time and no guarantees.

If your organization is in Southern California, the Southern California Broadcasters Association (SCBA) acts as a clearinghouse for nonprofit organizations. For a small fee, they assign file numbers that stations like to see at the bottom of all PSAs. Stations will accept material without an SCBA number, but distribution is easier and more effective with it. The process to get a number takes about two weeks. In other parts of the country there are state broadcasters' associations, but they do not have a public service arm. It would be useful to call the association for a list of radio and television stations and their public service directors. Then, independently, contact the stations to get detailed information. It is important to make sure that stations have all the information about your nonprofit status, including your IRS tax-exempt letter, a fact sheet on your company, and a press release on the event you are promoting. (See Figure 10.3.)

It is also important that your PSAs or "spots" be as professionally prepared as possible and that they be received by the stations at least two weeks before the first day you would like them to be aired.

Here are some tips from SCBA on writing your announcement:

- Remember that broadcasting is salesmanship
- Try to overcome your listeners' apathy and motivate them to do something
- Determine the objective/specific goal of the spot
- List all the pertinent facts to be included in order of their importance and then decide on the single most important thing you want to say
- Think about how you would say it if you were talking face-to-face with a person and then write it that way

Writing the spot:

1. Spots are generally ten, twenty, or thirty seconds long. Seldom if ever do sixty-second PSAs get aired. The approximate word count is as follows: ten seconds equals twenty words, twenty seconds equals fifty words, thirty seconds equals seventy-five words.
2. To be accurate, use a stopwatch.
3. Use 8 1/2" × 11" plain white paper.
4. Put only one announcement on a page.
5. Make it clear, clean copy. Use upper and lower case and double space.
6. Do not hyphenate at the end of a line and do not use abbreviations.
7. Include a telephone number and state it twice.
8. Do not mention prices.

After you write your announcement:

1. Read it aloud. Is it timed correctly? Does it sound natural or stilted?

2. Did you grab the listener's attention right away?
3. Did you deliver the main message clearly and quickly? Will the listener remember?
4. Did you mention the key facts? Did you mention both the name of the organization and the telephone number at least twice?
5. Did you urge the listener to take an action?
6. Was the spot interesting?

Each public service announcement must include:

- The full legal name and complete address of your dance group
- The name, title and phone number of your contact person
- When to start and when to end the announcements (dates)
- The announcer's reading time (carefully timed)
- The message
- The SCBA file number if you have one

Once your PSAs meet all these standards, mail them flat to the public service director of the station. When dealing with television you will also need a glass-mounted color slide or a videotape. Check with your local television station for the exact requirements. As your budget grows you may be able to produce audiotapes and video-tapes for radio and television, but at first you will send live copy to radio and slides and live copy to television stations. "Live" copy means that an announcer from the station will read the copy.

Public affairs shows

These programs are also good outlets to get exposure on the air-waves. Both radio and television have local shows that might be appropriate for your dance company. Cable channels in particular have numerous local shows that might want to interview you or one of your dancers.

It is always a good idea to monitor any show that you are inter-ested in. Note the interviewer's topics, approach, and style; in other words, learn the show's format. Keep in mind the news value of your dance company and how it may relate to a particular show. Once you are familiar with the format, send a pitch letter and outline why your dance company or a dancer or choreographer may be a good subject for the show. Include a fact sheet on the company, a press release, and a brochure, if available. Follow up with a telephone call. Often, the booker of the show has not yet read your letter or has read it and not yet decided if your idea is appropriate. The telephone call is your second chance to "sell" your idea.

Once you have set an interview, send a confirming letter with a bio on the interviewee. Sometimes it is helpful if you send a list of suggested questions, particularly if the host is not very familiar with dance. Make sure that both your interviewer and interviewee have the same information (i.e., copies of the pitch letter, bio, fact sheet, and suggested questions). Always accompany your interviewees to the station to ensure that they do not get lost or lose their nerve, and are on time. These tips hold true for print interviews as well, although most print reporters you pitch would not like to get suggested questions because, unlike broadcast media generalists, they pride themselves on doing their research and being prepared. After the show has aired, send a letter of thanks and include any reactions you received to the program. For example, if the box office got lots of calls, say so. Stations are vitally interested in program response. This type of follow-up strengthens relationships and enhances your chances of setting up future shows. (Newspaper reporters do not have the same type of pressure for rating. Nevertheless, a thank you after a story appears can be a nice gesture.)

Other promotions

A ticket give-away promotion is another way to get attention on the radio. I am sure you have heard these offers being made many times: the tenth caller will receive a pair of tickets to such and such. You can set up those types of give-aways by working with the promotion department of a radio station. You can do it on a few stations at the same time. It is an inexpensive way to get air time that would otherwise be out of your budget.

A "photo opportunity" you dream up may get both the broadcast and the print media to attend. For example, you may decide to do a special mini-performance in the children's ward of a hospital. You would work with the public relations department of the hospital. The media attention could be advantageous for both the hospital and your company. This would be true in a retirement home or a shopping mall as well. You just need to be creative. Once you settle on the event and have carefully worked out all the details, invite the media to attend.

Contact: Sam Dawson
The Hot Shot Dance Company   September 11, 1997
(310) 765-4321

Memo For Coverage

WHO: The Hot Shot Dance Company

WHAT: Open Rehearsal of Jazz Ditty (which will have its premiere

            opening night, Tuesday, September 23 at City Theatre.)

When: Thursday, September 18, 1997 at 10:30 a.m.

Where: "Shall We Dance" Dance Studio
            1234 Darling Lane, Anywhere, Ca.

Photo opportunity for television and still photographers as well as

opportunity for press interviews with Director/choreographer Bill Smith and the

dancers. Smith and the Hot Shot Dance Company have played to packed

houses throughout Europe and the United States. Bill has chosen to premiere

"Jazz Ditty" in our City because, it was here that he got his first break as a

dancer when he was spotted by Merce Cunningham in a college dance concert.

The rest is history.

Please RSVP to: Sam Dawson (310) 765-4321

Figure 10.4 Memo for coverage.

Coverage

Similar to a press release, a memo for coverage (Figure 10.4) is set up with facts that are easy to grasp: who, what, when, and where as well as additional details such as what spokesperson will be available. That is it. The memo for coverage is then faxed or mailed to the news desk of television stations and to reporters who would cover dance events. You follow up your memo with a telephone call to see if the event will be covered. Often, you are told they plan to cover the event, but do not be surprised if no one shows up because a fire or murder took precedence. Such things happen at least once in the life of a publicist.

Figure 10.5 Sample flier.

MARKETING MATERIALS

Flyers

Simple single sheets, usually $8\,1/2'' \times 5\,1/2''$ (one half of an $8\,1/2'' \times 11''$ piece of paper), flyers (Figure 10.5) are easy and inexpensive to create. They are usually produced on colored stock with black ink and can be left in bunches at libraries, student lounges, senior citizen homes, and so forth. They announce the event and have the time, place, ticket information, and where to call. The flyer may also include graphics and a quote or two from your best reviews.

Window cards

Printed on card stock, window cards (Figure 10.6) are slightly more costly than flyers but are more easily seen. The poster should feature a great photo or graphic and all the flyer information. With permission, they can be posted in the windows of local stores, at the site where your company is performing, and any other place where people congregate.

Mailing lists

A mailing list is very important when it comes to developing and building an audience for your performances. When you first start, try to borrow mailing lists from other arts organizations, pay for lists from mailing houses, and gather every name and address you can from any other sources or persons that show interest in your company. At your performances, ask the audience to fill out information cards so that you can add them to your list. It is the life blood of your audience development and should be built and managed with care. All the general publicity in the world is not as effective as word-of-mouth or a list of people who are genuinely interested in your dance performances.

Keep your company in the public eye even when you are not getting ready for a performance. Your board may do a fundraising event to which you invite the society press. You may have the company do free performances at schools or festivals. Each event is an opportunity for some exposure not only to the media but to the general public. At such events, gather names and addresses of those interested in being on your mailing list.

Computers have revolutionized the ability to keep press lists and to be able to mass mail. Even the most basic computer is far more efficient than yesterday's typewriter. Fax machines, too, make getting information disseminated quickly far easier than with messengers. Sometimes a reporter will want information from you quickly and a fax machine or e-mail capability is helpful, but remember not to fax or e-mail unwanted information to the media. They find it intrusive and are put off by "pushy" publicists. It is better to ask if

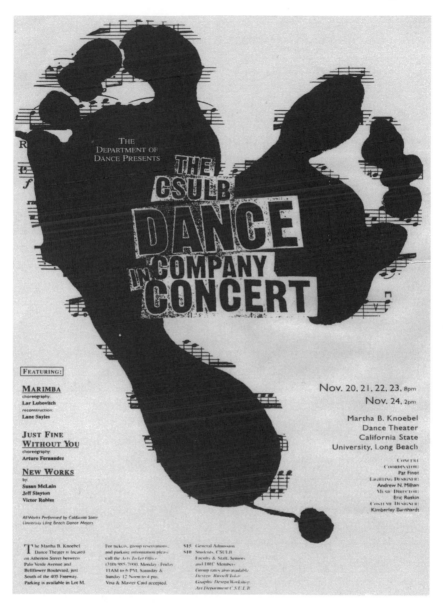

Figure 10.6 Poster (window card).

you might fax or e-mail before doing so. We all hear about the World Wide Web and "web sites." It seems that everyone has one. But the question is, who really looks at web sites for their decisions on going to a dance concert? Certainly, if you know how to or have a friend willing to create a web site for you, do it. But it is not a priority and may not pay off in any appreciable manner.

CONCERT AND POSTCONCERT

You have gotten some advance publicity in the newspaper and on radio and television. Now it is time to invite dance critics to attend your event. It is a good idea to send a simple letter of invitation requesting their presence and asking that they RSVP. When they accept the invitation, tell them that the tickets will be at a press table, particularly if it is opening night. You can leave tickets at the box office for the press as well, but it is preferable to have a press table on opening night where you hand out the tickets, along with a program and a press kit. This is your opportunity to meet press people and establish that all-important rapport. The press kit for the evening should include specific information on the evening's program, a general release about the group or company, and bios on the dancers. Black and white photographs should be made available and given to the press who request them.

In addition to critics, invite anyone who did a story for you prior to the event, any press that you are trying to cultivate for the future, and any behind-the-scenes people, such as bookers of shows or the public service director that made sure your PSA was aired. These people are often just as important as the critic. Be sure to give every press person a complimentary pair of tickets for good seats. The best seats, of course, are for the critics, but all the seats should be good. The investment will pay off many times over in the future.

Often, larger newspapers will send their own photographer to your opening night. Prior to the event, decide just where the photographer can locate so that he or she can get the best shots. Accompany the photographer to that spot and make sure you provide whatever is needed. The photographer should have a press kit or a program to identify the dance and dancers.

Tell critics that you will be available in the lobby at intermission to answer any questions, and should there be any change in the program it is up to you to find the critics and give them updated information. To facilitate your contact with the attending media, keep a press list with seat assignments with you at all times.

Remember that the press is powerful. Make it your ally. It can make or break your run. You want to treat its representatives with kid gloves and accommodate their wishes, even if it is an inconvenience to you. A word of caution: other than offering to be available or to inform a critic about a program change, *leave them alone.* They do not want to be personally involved with you when they are trying to review.

Good reviews are wonderful tools. Paste up your best reviews on good 8" × 11" paper (sometimes it will require larger paper, but try to make it easy to fold). Include the actual newspaper banner or name of the paper as well as the date of the publication. Include your reviews in your press kits. Use them for fundraising. Post them in the lobby or window of the performance site. Use quotes from the reviews in your brochures, flyers, window cards, and fundraising literature. There is nothing so wonderful as someone else saying your company is terrific. When you use a quote in your printed materials be sure to get permission from the newspaper and the writer and that you credit both correctly.

As your program/company grows, marketing opportunities will present themselves. It is your responsibility to capitalize on any opportunity to get your name and your company before the public. Be alert, be thinking, be creative, and be ready. If you have a good product and make marketing a priority, you will be successful in building and retaining an audience.

11 . Fundraising: An Overview

LAURIE DOWLING *Director for Women's Enterprise Development Corporation. Los Angeles-based nonprofit manager in development and fundraising for the arts. Development Director for Peter Sellars, Los Angeles Festival.*

This chapter is designed to give you, the artist, manager, director, or board member, suggestions on how to reconcile yourself to and embrace the fundraising, or development process, and some initial thoughts on how to go about it.

WHO MAY FUNDRAISE?

Individuals, companies, and foundations may make tax-deductible donations to your activities if you are a nonprofit organization registered with the Federal (and in California, the State) government. Most arts organizations are 501(c)3 nonprofit corporations that are allowed to take tax-deductible contributions because their activities are perceived to operate "for the public benefit."

If you are an individual artist planning a dance concert and not operating under the auspices of a nonprofit organization, you cannot just solicit donations by yourself. You are required by law to have a "fiscal receiver," a nonprofit organization that is willing to accept donations on your behalf, administer the funds, and report to funders that the activity proceeded as promised from an artistic and fiscal standpoint. Most individual artists undertake concerts or exhibitions in collaboration with a fiscal receiver (if they are not commissioned and paid directly by a nonprofit organization). In Los Angeles and most areas, there are a number of organizations that are willing to act as a fiscal receiver on a project-by-project basis. Check with your local arts services organizations, your university, or other nonprofits of which you are aware. Most will accept, although some will request a small percentage of the amount received to cover their administrative time, a fiscal receiver's fee.

WHY FUNDRAISE?

Yes, this may seem obvious. You have to have the money. But that is not the whole story. Let us look at why people fundraise, so that you can feel comfortable with undertaking the activity. You fundraise for one main reason: to be able to support and share the compelling artistic vision that drives you to create or execute dance. If this reason is not compelling enough for you to overcome your natural reluctance to ask people to support your activity with money, you are probably in the wrong field. If you do not have enough faith in your own vision and talent to ask people to help you realize it, you may not have enough confidence in yourself as an artist to execute it, either.

If you are raising money so that you can share your vision, how is that "begging"? It is not, not if you believe in your vision. What you are doing is one of the most exciting things you can do. You are giving individuals, corporations, or foundations the chance to take part in your exciting project. It is beneficial to you (that vision thing), the community (they are the audience who will love it), and to the funders (they are taking part in a wonderful journey that will benefit the community and themselves). So you see, it is a good thing!

WHERE TO GO FOR MONEY

The real answer to fundraising success is (1) find a method that works within your style, and (2) continue to develop a base of contacts that support your growth as an artist or as a company. Use existing sources for your research. University libraries usually have access to the Foundation Center Library on-line. This lists compilations of corporate and foundation funding sources. In Los Angeles, the California Community Foundation's Funding Information Center provides free training in how to use their library, and also has access to information on private family foundations as well as larger, more traditional ones. Most other communities have similar research facilities at community foundations or the local public library.

Start with your family. For our purposes, we will include your friends in this category. In other words, your first line of resource should be the people who already know that you do good work and are a talented artist. These are friends, neighbors, former employers, and businesses with which you have some relationship. Try asking them to help you first. This will do two things: (1) it gets you some early success—a good thing; (2) it gives you a "leadership" commitment that may be matched by other funders. Individuals can also be guides to other sources of funding, such as matching gifts from their corporations or referrals to contacts at corporations or potential individual donors.

HOW TO ASK

Individuals

Ask individuals in person if at all possible. This lets you present your compelling reasons for support in a clear and passionate way, and you can get a strong sense of how the individual is responding at all times. Have a meeting with the person you are soliciting (preferably with a board member or other friendly contact on hand) and present your request directly to the potential funder. If this is impossible, the next method is to send a clear, concise, and compelling letter that is then followed up by telephone.

Remember, it is important to martial your facts and present them clearly enough so that the reasons for your request, and the benefits to the community and the potential donor, are easy to follow. Use the "Who, What, When, Where, Why" rule. "Who" is the support for? "What" will happen and "what" are you asking for? "When" is the event? "Where" will it take place? "Why" is it important to the community, and this potential donor? After you present the facts and ask for support, you may not receive an answer immediately. (In fact, you would probably prefer that they think about your request.) Be sure to indicate how you plan to follow up (telephone call or letter) and do so when you say you will. After you receive the support, thank each donor and continue to keep them up-to-speed on how you are progressing. In the main, successful development is doing what our mothers taught us: thanking people, being solicitous of their comfort, and continuing to express our appreciation for their part in our ongoing activities. Basically, it is just good manners.

A note about backup materials: usually it is appropriate to have all requests for support accompanied by some general information on the organization, a copy of the 501(c)3 certification, general financial material, and a business card of the contact person.

Corporations

Corporate support is usually thought of as big sponsorship money: "Masterpiece Theatre is made possible in part by the Mobil

Corporation." This is true. However, corporate support may also come from the local donut shop where you and your dancers have been pigging out for three years. Or it may come in the form of donated printing for your program and posters from the copy shop you worked at last summer. Be creative in whom you approach and what you ask them for. Just remember the real rule of corporate fundraising: ask them for something they will want to give and for an amount that makes it possible for them to say "yes."

In-kind donations are donations of goods or services made usually by corporations and sometimes by individuals. These may include providing food for receptions or events, printing, office equipment, or pro bono legal help. In-kind is as good as cash, as long as you really need what you're being offered. A thousand diapers may not be useful if you do not serve toddlers, but a free run of stationery and business cards can be a wonderful thing. In-kind can come from many sources, some of which may also give you cash. Many large corporations are willing to undertake printing for nonprofits. Most law firms have some program for *pro bono* services; some accounting firms do as well. It is often less painful for corporations to give in-kind than cash, so do not forget this possibility when you are soliciting for support from local companies.

Corporations usually want to have your request in writing and they are usually willing to tell you how to present it. In other words, if they are interested in hearing more from you, whether they are the large corporation or the local print shop they will ask you to put your request in writing. This is only appropriate and it also makes it easier to ensure that everyone understands what is being requested and why.

Again, make sure your request document is clear, concise, and compelling. Also, carefully articulate what kind of recognition or benefit the corporation will get from participation. This will help to ensure that there are no missed communications during the course of your relationship.

Foundations

Traditional, large foundations (e.g., Ford, Rockefeller, Irvine) usually have formal application procedures and seriously long lead times. They also seldom fund an individual artist's project or smaller events. However, there are a number of private family foundations in every state that do just that. They can give answers far more rapidly, especially if a relatively small amount of money is involved.

Private family foundations are usually started for two reasons: for tax breaks for reasonably wealthy individuals or families; to allow people to help their community in a way that makes sense within their personal interests and philanthropic instincts. You would be surprised at how many people you may know who have family foundations.

Foundations usually have very clear procedures for requesting support. Follow them to the letter. If they ask for ten typewritten copies of the application form, make sure that you send the ten copies and that you typed the application. Again, the clear, concise, and compelling rule applies. State your case as clearly and passionately as you can, explaining why this foundation should select your project from among the thousands they receive annually. Prior to sending a request, be sure to read the guidelines and try to communicate with the program officer, if it is allowed (some foundations intentionally are unable to allow program officers to communicate with would-be grantees in advance of being considered for an award). After sending the request, call to make sure it has been received and ask if they need any additional material. Make a follow-up call in a month or two after submitting a proposal to see if any additional material is needed or if the foundation staff has any questions.

Government

Another source of support, both for ongoing operations and specific projects, is government grants or contracts. These vary from state to state and from locality to locality. You will need to conduct research based on the unique possibilities offered by the arts councils in your region. The National Endowment for the Arts has limited resources for individuals and small organizations but should be contacted to see if support is feasible.

Another source of government support is contracts. Many municipalities contract with artists or organizations to provide certain services, for example, for in-school or holiday performances or training. These are contracts for services, not grants, and are usually bid through a "request for proposals" process. Some municipalities and states also implement certain incentives for organizations and activities that bring people and revenues into economically distressed neighborhoods. You may wish to investigate the options in your community.

Special events

Many artists and organizations undertake a variety of special events to raise funds for projects or ongoing operations. They are often labor intensive, especially those that are elaborate in nature, such as black-tie dinners, but they have the added benefit of increasing visibility of the project or organization. Whatever you select should reflect your project or organization as much as possible. Look at what other organizations are doing to avoid too much repetition. One organization sells holiday greenery around its performances of *The Nutcracker*. Another hosts an annual bowling party in which local celebrities pair with community members. The other key point in a special event is to undertake research to make sure your pricing is within what the market will bear. Take a look at what other organizations are charging for similar events and conduct an informal poll of some of your loyal supporters to see what they would be willing to pay for your event of choice.

WHERE TO GO FROM HERE

The above are basic suggestions about how to get started in your quest for resources that will help to make your vision a reality. You will want to adapt them to fit the unique strengths of your organization or group of supporters. What is truly important is to find a method of requesting support that works for you and build on it. A primary rule of fundraising: there is a pleasurable way for everyone to participate. It is up to you to find it for each member of your organization's team. The important thing is to bring the same creativity that you use in building your art to looking for ways to fund it. Your major strength as artists is your ability to adapt and to think on (or with) your feet. This makes you ideal fundraisers, if you just get underway.

Bibliography

GENERAL

Elder, Eldon. *Will It Make a Theatre?* NY: Off-Off Broadway Alliance, 1979.

Ellfeldt, Lois. *Dance Production.* Palo Alto, CA: National Press Books, 1971.

Green, Joann. *The Small Theatre Handbook: A Guide to Management and Production.* Harvard, MA: The Harvard Common Press, 1981.

Hayes, Elizabeth, et al. *A Guide to Dance Production.* Reston, VA: National Dance Association, 1981.

Horosko, Marian, and Judith R.F. Kupersmith. *The Dancer's Survival Manual.* NY: Harper & Row, 1987.

Papolos, Janice. *Performing Artist's Handbook.* Cincinnati, OH: Writer's Digest Books, 1984.

Performing Arts Directory 1988 (issued annually). NY: Dance Magazine, 1987.

White, David, executive ed. *Poor Dancer's Almanac: A Survival Manual for Choreographers, Managers and Dancers.* NY: Dance Theater Workshop, 1983.

CHAPTER 2

David, Martin A. *The Dancer's Audition Book.* New York: Sterling Publishing Company, 1982.

Dunkel, Stuart Edward. *The Audition Process: Anxiety Management and Coping Strategies.* Stuyvesant, NY: Pendragon Press, 1989.

Nielsen, Eric Brandt. *Dance Auditions: Preparation, Presentation, Career Planning.* Princeton, NJ: Princeton Book Company, Publishers, 1984.

CHAPTER 3

Bellman, Willard F. *Scene Design, Stage Lighting, Sound, Costume, and Makeup: A Scenographic Approach.* New York: Harper & Row, 1983.

Gillette, A.S. *Stage Scenery: Its Construction and Rigging.* New York: Harper & Row, 1981.

Gruver, Bert, and Frank Hamilton. *The Stage Manager's Handbook.* New York: Drama Book Specialists, 1979.

Stern, Lawrence. *Stage Management.* 2nd ed. Boston: Allyn and Bacon, 1987.

Sweet, Harvey. *Handbook of Scenery, Properties and Lighting.* Vol. 2. 2nd ed. Needham Heights, MA: Allyn and Bacon, 1995.

Wilfred, Thomas. *Project Scenery: A Technical Manual.* New York: Drama Book Specialists, 1987.

CHAPTER 4

Burris-Meyer, Harold, Vincent Mallory, and Lewis Goodfellow. *Sound in the Theatre.* New York: Theatre Arts Books, 1979.

Eargle, John. *Sound Recording.* 2nd ed. New York: Van Nostrand Reinhold, 1980.

Grant, Donald J. *A History of Western Music.* New York: W. W. Norton & Co., 1986.

Randel, Don, ed. *The Harvard Dictionary of Music.* Cambridge, MA: Harvard University Press, 1986.

Runstein, Robert E. and David Miles Huber. *Modern Recording Techniques.* 2nd ed. Indianapolis: Howard W. Sams, 1986.

Teck, Katherine. *Ear Training for the Body; A Dancer's Guide to Music.* Pennington, NJ: Princeton Book Company, Publishers, 1994.

———. *Movement to Music: Musicians in the Dance Studio.* Westport, CT: Greenwood Press, 1990.

———. *Music for the Dance: Reflections on a Collaborative Art.* Westport, CT: Greenwood Press, 1989.

Woram, John M. *The Recording Studio Handbook.* Plainview, NY: Elar Publishing Co., 1982.

CHAPTER 5

Bentley, Toni. *Costumes by Karinska.* New York: Harry Abrams, Inc., 1995.

Emery, Joy Spanabel. *Stage Costume Techniques.* Englewood Cliffs, NJ: Prentice-Hall, 1981.

Harrison, Mary Kent. *How to Dress Dancers: Costuming Techniques for Dance.* Princeton, NJ: Princeton Book Company, Publishers, 1988.

Holkeboer, Katherine Strand. *Patterns for Theatrical Costumes: Garments, Trims, and Accessories From Ancient Egypt to 1915.* Englewood Cliffs, NJ: Prentice-Hall, 1984.

Ingham, Rosemary, and Covey, Liz. *The Costume Designer's Handbook: A Complete Guide for Amateur and Professional Costume Designers.* Englewood Cliffs, NJ: Prentice-Hall, 1983.

Jackson, Carole. *Color Me Beautiful.* New York: Ballantine Books, 1980.

Strong, Roy, Ivor Guest, Richard Buckle, Barry Kay, and Liz de Costa. *Designing for the Dancer*; foreword by Dame Alicia Markova. London : Elron Press, 1981.

Yarwood, Doreen. *Encyclopedia of World Costume.* New York : Charles Scribner's Sons, 1978.

CHAPTER 6

Bentham, Frederick. *The Art of Stage Lighting.* New York: Theatre Arts Books, 1976.

Gillette, J. Michael. *Designing with Light.* 2nd ed. Palo Alto, CA: Mayfield Publishing Co., 1989.

Palmer, Richard H. *The Lighting Art.* 2nd ed. Englewood Cliffs, NJ: Prentice–Hall, 1994.

Parker, W. Oren, Harvey K. Smith, and R. Craig Wolf. *Scene Design and Stage Lighting.* 5th ed. New York: Holt, Rinehart and Winston, 1985.

Pilbrow, Richard. *Stage Lighting.* New York: Drama Book Specialists, 1979.

Rosenthal, Jean, and Lael Wertenbaker. *The Magic of Light.* Boston: Little, Brown and Company, 1972.

Sweet, Harvey. *Handbook of Scenery, Properties, and Lighting.* Vol. 2. 2nd ed. Needham Heights, MA: Allyn & Bacon, 1995.

Watson, Lee. *Lighting Design Handbook.* New York: McGraw-Hill, 1990.

CHAPTER 7

Felici, James. *Desktop Publishing Skills.* Reading, MA: Addison-Wesley, 1988.

Levine, Mindy N. and Susan Frank. *Get Me To The Printer . . . On Time, On or Under Budget, and Looking Good.* New York: Off-Off Broadway Alliance, 1988.

CHAPTER 8

Arnink, Donna J. *Creative Theatrical Makeup.* Englewood Cliffs, NJ: Prentice-Hall, 1984.

Carsons, Richard. *Stage Makeup.* 8th ed. Englewood Cliffs, NJ: Prentice-Hall, 1990.

Corey, Irene. *The Face is a Canvas.* New Orleans: Anchorage Press, Inc., 1990.

————. *The Mask of Reality: An Approach to Design for Theatre.* New Orleans: Anchorage Press, 1968.

Diakonoff, Serge. *Metamorphoses.* Dell'arte Publications, 1984.

Siegmund, W. Christian, ed. *Modern Mask Design.* Hamburg, Germany: Siegmund-Verlag, 1986.

CHAPTER 9

Cavanaugh, Jim. *Organization and Management of Non-Professional Theatre.* New York: Richards Rosen Press, Inc., 1973.

Farber, Donald. *A Guide to Producing Plays Off-Broadway.* New York: Drama Book Specialists, 1988.

Langley, Stephen. *Theatre Management and Production in America.* New York: Drama Book Publishers, 1990.

Reid, Francis. *Theatre Administration.* London: A & C Black Publishers Ltd., 1983.

CHAPTER 10

Klein, Ted, and Fred Danzig. *Publicity: How to Make the Media Work for You.* New York: Charles Scribner's Sons, 1985.

Newman, Danny. *Subscribe Now! Building an Audience Through Dynamic Subscription Promotion.* New York: Theatre Communications Group, 1977.

Rados, David L. *Marketing for Nonprofit Organizations.* Boston: Auburn House Publishing Company, 1981.

Reiss, Alvin. *The Arts Management Handbook.* New York: Law-Arts Publishers, 1986.

CHAPTER 11

Edles, L. Peter. *Fundraising: Hands-on Tactics for Nonprofit Groups.* New York: McGraw-Hill, 1993.

Reiss, Alvin H. *Cash In! Funding and Promoting the Arts.* New York: Theatre Communications Group, 1986.

Stolper, Carolyn. *Successful Fundraising for Arts and Cultural Organizations.* Phoenix, AZ: Oryx Press, 1989.

Glossary

Apron: Part of the stage floor extending beyond the proscenium arch into the auditorium; forestage.

Batten: A length of rigid material, usually pipe or wood, on which lights or scenery are hung.

Beams, antepro or F O H (front of house): Position for lighting equipment in auditorium in front of the proscenium.

Bias: A line diagonal to the grain of a fabric. When cut at a slant to the selvage the fabric is less stable, since many threads are left on the raw edge.

Boom: A vertical pipe screwed into a very heavy steel base, commonly positioned in the wings, used to hang instruments for medium- and low-angle side lights. Also called a tree or floor stand.

Border: A horizontal masking curtain, hung over the stage to mask the lights and the flies.

Box boom: A front of the house lighting position in the side wall of the auditorium. Also called side wall slot.

Call-back: An invitation to return for another audition.

Casing: The edge of the fabric at the waistline, cuff, hemline, or leg hole that is folded over and sewn to allow room to insert a string or elastic.

Color media or color filters: Transparent materials such as glass, gelatin, or sheet plastic placed in holders at the front of a lighting instrument to produce a colored light. Often referred to as "gel," a slang term for gelatin, which was the original product but which is no longer manufactured.

Cyclorama (cyc): Stage backdrop, sometimes U-shaped; neutral or light color, used for sky effects.

Deadwood: Unsold tickets.

Decibel: A measure of loudness intensity.

Diffuse: To gently tap and blend makeup so that there are no hard edges.

Electric: Any batten on which stage lighting instruments are hung.

Fade: To gradually lessen the amount of makeup color.

Fiscal receiver: A nonprofit organization that serves an individual artist by accepting, administering, and reporting on donations.

501 (C)3: Government number assigned to nonprofit, tax-exempt organizations.

Flat: Wooden frame covered with canvas, used as a scenic unit. It may be from ten to twenty feet in height and in varying widths.

Flies: Space above the dancing-acting area in which scenery can be flown for storage.

Flying: Shifting scenery by raising it vertically over the dancing-acting area by rope line rigging or the counterweight system. The fastest and quietest method of shifting.

Gelatin (gel): See Color media.

Ground row: The scenic element that masks the lighting instruments that light the bottom of a cyclorama or backdrop. Sometimes, ground row masking. Also, the name for the lighting instruments used for this purpose.

Gusset: An extra triangle of fabric at the armhole or crotch of a garment that allows for extra movement.

Hardwood: Special passes, vouchers, or complimentary tickets.

Heads up, headache: Words of caution that are used to warn people on stage of dangerous circumstances on stage.

Highlight: To accentuate a feature with makeup.

Jacks: See Plugs

Leader tape: Paper or plastic tape, the same width as recording tape, used to separate sections of recorded tape.

Legs: Set of draperies used to mask the backstage area from the audience.

Light plot: A plan view of the stage that shows the exact location of all lighting instruments and details the channel number, dimmer number, instrument type, wattage, color, number, and sometimes focus, for each.

Lighting rehearsal: The rehearsal at which the lighting designer composes the actual light cues for the dance with the choreographer and all dancers present and in costume.

Magic sheet: A diagram used by lighting designers listing important information from the light plot—generally angle, focus, channel numbers, and color—in a condensed fashion for quick reference.

Masking: Placing either framed or unframed scenery in a position to prevent the audience from seeing the backstage area.

Overlock: Sewing machine with three or four threads that finishes the edge of the fabric as it sews.

Patch cables (audio): Cords equipped on both ends with some kind of connector used to connect electrical equipment, such as a cable connecting a tape recorder to an amplifier.

Patchboard (audio): A panel containing many input or output jacks that can be wired together.

Patching (audio): The connecting of one electrical apparatus to another with jacks or plugs.

Plugs (jacks): Connecting device for tape recorders, phonographs, and electrical equipment (Figure 4.1).

Proscenium arch: Frame around the opening of the stage.

Rigging: All of the activities associated with the initial assembly of a setting when it is first taken to the stage. Rigging also readies a set to be shifted.

Romantic tutu: A long ballet costume with approximately six layers of tulle in the skirt and a fitted bodice with the skirt extending below the knees or to the ankles. First worn by Marie Taglioni in *La Sylphide* in 1832.

Scaled theatre: A theatre in which the seats are sold at different prices.

Scrim: A finely woven netting with a rectangular weave through which light may or may not be seen, depending on how it is lit. May be hung as a backdrop or as a curtain between audience and performers.

Selvage: Edge of a fabric that is woven so that it will not fray or ravel.

Set: A unit of scenery.

Shade: To change slightly the degree of shadow color.

Shadow: To make a feature less noticeable.

Spike mark: To mark the position of a set piece or person on the stage floor, usually with colored tape.

Spill: Unwanted light from a poorly focused or shuttered spotlight.

Splicing (editing): Joining together two pieces of recording tape or leader tape using a short piece of splicing tape.

Stage walker: A stand-in for the performer during a cue-to-cue lighting rehearsal.

Strike: To clear the stage; remove scenery and props, for example.

Tack: Large, loose stitch used as a temporary binding, or as a marker.

Tech rehearsal: A rehearsal at which the technical aspects of the production are integrated.

Ticket manifest: The seating plan of a theatre.

Traveler curtain: A curtain that opens to the side.

Tutu: A costume with a fitted bodice on a ballet skirt that stands out straight around the hips. It is made from approximately twelve layers of mixed tulle and net, depending on the desired stiffness of the skirt. Usually there are from twelve to fourteen inches of length in the top layer of the skirt.

Unitard: Leotard and tights combined into a one piece, skin tight, stretch garment.

Wings: Space outside the performing area at the right and left of the stage. Draperies that hang at the side of the stage to mask the offstage areas.

Index